NAH! WE WRITERS HAVE TOO MUCH IMAGINATION. WE THINK THE READER'S EVERYWHERE. I'LL JUST TURN UP THE LIGHTS AND GET BACK TO WORK...

AH! THAT'S THE TITLE PAGE DONE... BUT IS IT ZAPPY ENOUGH TO GRAB THE READING PUBLIC?
CRISS-CROS
A TEXT BOOK OF MODERN COMPOSITION
JOHN RIDDELL
COACH HOUSE PRESS 1977

Criss-Cross was previously published in Ganglia 5 (1967);
Pope Leo: El Elope in The Cosmic Chef (1970);
The Bottle in Descant (1974);
an earlier version of Morox in Kontakte I (1976);
The Difference in The Story So Four (1976).

Cover sequence by John Ligoure.

Edited for the Press by bpNichol.

Set in Bodoni and printed in Canada
in an edition of 1000 copies at
The Coach House Press,
401 (rear) Huron Street,
Toronto, Canada M5S 2G5

Published with the assistance of the Canada Council
and the Ontario Arts Council.

ISBN 88910-025-x

'Prudery alone can no longer effectively censor imaginative writing, but 'editorial discretion' can, especially if censor taboos are pervasive in the business – for instance, that currently proscribing pronounced stylistic originality, especially in its more difficult forms, and those prohibiting predominately visual fiction.'

– Richard Kostelanetz
Breakthrough Fictioneers
1972

a note on form

during this century traditional & avant garde literature have each virtually polarized around what i call two dogmas of literality

traditionalists will admit no textform other than linear into the arena will consider experimentation to be valid only if conducted fundamentally within this frame of reference

the avant garde find the traditional approach to composition too exclusive will consider experimentation to be valid within any frame

a synthesis may not be desired / is certainly not effected by displaying both schools under the same roof still when brot together the prospect of marriage does not seem as remote as may have been supposed

'criss-cross' is meant to entertain offers a variety of compositional techniques hopefully will stimulate discussion & furthur explorations in the field nor is it difficult to foresee such explorations extending into novel areas

jhr

'While music and the plastic arts and poetry painfully dug themselves out of the inadequate dogmas of 19th century 'realism,' by a passionate commitment to the idea of progress in art and a hectic quest for new idioms and new materials, the novel has proved unable to assimilate whatever of genuine quality and spiritual ambition has been performed in its name in the 20th century. It has sunk to the level of an art form deeply, if not irrevocably, compromised by philistinism.'

– Susan Sontag
Against Interpretation
1965

for bpNichol
steve mccaffery
bill bissett

Criss-Cross

Sequence # 1: pre-work (8AM - 9AM)

Well

```
r r r r r r r r r r r r r r r r r
r                 r               r
r                 r               r
r                 r               r
r                 r               r
r                 r               r
r                 r               r
r               r                 r
r         r r r                   r
r r r r                           r
r                                 r
r                                 r
r r r r r r r r r r r r r r r r r
```

he

1

gets

```
m m m m m m m m m m m m m m m m m m m m m m m m m m m m m m
 m                                                      m
  m                                                    m
   m      P  H  I  L  I  P                            m
    m     T Y P E   S C  7 9 6 0                     m      SPEED - FLEX 800
     m                                              m
      m                                            m
       m                                          m
        m                                        m
         m           110V = AC/DC               m
          m                                    m
           m                                  m
            m                                m
             m         12W 20'              m
              m                            m
PHILISHAVE     m                          m
                m    MADE IN HOLLAND     m
                 m                      m
                  m m m m m m m m m m m
```

up

2

a) KREST

the only toothpaste
with
fluoridine,
tested
and found
effective
against cavities.

leading dental journals report:
21%
to
49%
fewer cavities
with Krest,

in more than 13 years
of independant
of independant clinical
of independant clinical tests

on
adults
and
children

b) FEEL REALLY CLEAN, REFRESHED! d b
e e
.Positive decdorant action o a
d Z u
.Mild, gentle lather o I t
r P y
.No unsightly bathtub ring a b
n a
t r

in

c) V N Triple A

Natural helathy looking hair with just seconds of care is yours with V N Triple A. Lanolin-rich, concentrated VN Triple A penetrates each hair shaft, gives new life and lustre to dull dry hair, makes hair easy to comb and manage, even after shampoos. Not sticky or greasy

the

d)

water
resistant
K I W I BLACK
leather
nourishing

e)

Vitamin A......5000 Int

Vitamin D...... 500 Int

Vitamin B^1...... 3 mg

Vitamin B^6...... 1 mg

ONE
A
DAY
MULTIPLE
VITAMINS

Riboflavin...... 2.5 mg

Vitamin C ...... 40 mg

Niacinamide.....20 mg

Vitamin B^{12}.....3 mcg

morning,

INSERT COINS

I n s e r t e x a c t a m o u n t
o f
n i c k l e s d i m e s q u a r t e r s

PRESS BRAND DESIRED

A l l b r a n d s 4 0 ¢

And

(Minors forbidden to
operate this machine)

he

"Well, what d'ya think Jim?"

"Tremendous! Picked 'er up last night, eh?"

"Yeah. I was gettin' a bit tired of the old stock. Took every cent I had to get this baby but it's worth it. What a machine! It's a factory rated 425 h p 396 Chevy engine equipped with an Edelbrock X-C96 dualquad log manifold, & an Isky 550 - 62 cam and kit; a gain of 71 hp at6,500 RPM over stock, and greater operating range."

goes

to

T R A N S

$$\text{HORSEPOWER} = \frac{\text{PLAN}}{33{,}000}$$

P O R T

work

P - mean effective pressure in lbs/sq"
L - length of stroke in '
A - piston area in sq "
N - number of cycles / min

A T I O N

at

Sequence # 2: work (9AM - 5PM)

1

"'Morning Jim."

"'Morning Tom. 'Morning Dick. 'Morning Harry."

Dull smiles of recognition from co-workers. Jim noticed three thin steel-caged columns of punch cards waiting by his desk. Familiar red plug-tape hung in loose, twisted shavings over the edge.

"What do you think of her?"

"Well, she laughs in the right places."

2

nine,

EXTRA
•
SUGAR

Press
&hold
Buttons

EXTRA
•
CREAM

coffee
with sugar
•

coffee
cream & sugar •

• coffee
black

tea •

• chocolate

•
coffee
with cream

Animal
Books
Communication
Drive
Explanation

Female
Genealogy
History
Imagination
Journalism
Killing

Love
Male
Nature
Observations
Politics
Quantity
Revolution
Sex
Time
Universe
Videotape
Want

X : criss-cross (disorientation; call program consultant)

Z : zig-zag (redistribute)

Gets

SHEET # 3,725

-(C)- -(P)- -(R)-
Specify: American Revolution
Required by: University of Toronto Library, Main

All information
Basic information
Particular information

(IBM digital computerex IKWR (Instantaneous Key Word Response) series 780(a)3, pre-programmed. Cardboard cards, pink, rectangular, chipped at the right-hand corner: (1) key-punch errors: if any, tape, reverse card and re-enter
(2) send output to decoding for final processing)

home

SHEET # 3,726

-(J)- -(C)- -( )-
Specify: in Canada
Required by: J. J. Sissons, Dept. Public Affairs, Ottawa 13, Canada.

All information
Basic information
Particular information

"Jim, there's another tray in run-off."

"Be right there Marj."

at

And

so awn

through

the

days,

weeks,

months...

five-thirty,

"'Night Jim."

"'Night Tom. 'Night Dick. 'Night Harry."

Sequence # 3: post-work (5PM - 12PM)

```
   s u b w a y

2 2 9 3 3 8 8 7 2
2               2
9    TORONTO    9
3    TRANSIT    3
3   AUTHORITY   3
8               8
8    16 2/3¢    8
7               7
2 2 9 3 3 8 8 7 2

   t o k e n
```

Takes

the

same

P A S S E N G E R S

must deposit own fare

O P E R A T O R

forbidden to do so

train

```
     008202           f
 up           down    a  t
                      r  o
 60 High Park 00      e
 50 Lansdowne 10            E
 40 Bathurst  20      p  z
 30 Yonge     30      a  o
 20 Broadview 40      i  n
 00 Danforth  60      d  e
```

every

time,

The operator of this vehicle has been carefully selected and trained for his duties. He is required to comply with the law & to operate his vehicle with due regard tothe comfort and safety of his passengers and other users of the road.

-Information Complex Center

Bank of Montreal- C

-Barber shop

Dominion-

-Ed's Variety

Jewellers-

O

-Woolworths

B A T H U R S T

Eatons-

L

-International Business Machines

Hudson's Furniture-

-Textiles

Cadet Cleaners-

L

S P A D I N A

-Esso

Restaraunt-

-Wolf's Mens Wear

E

Remo's-

-College Appliances

B A Y

Rack & Cue Billiards-

G

-Book Cellar

Record Bar-

-Teepee Tavern

E

Variety-

Y O N G E

B L
R A
E B
W LABATT'S A
E T
R T
S '
india S

S
I O
N IPA F
C
E C
pale ale A
1 N
8 A
2 D
8 A

3

INSERT COINS

I n s e r t e x a c t a m o u n t
o f
n i c k l e s d i m e s q u a r t e r s

PRESS BRAND DESIRED

A l l b r a n d s 4 0 ¢

(Minors forbidden to
operate this machine)

4

5 Choice: (a) go to hockey game?
(b) take girl freind to a movie?
(c) watch T.V.?
(d) go to the pub with "the guys"?

-(Z)- -(Z)- -(Z)-

6 No Choice: (a) pay rent
(b) eat
(c) sleep a little
(d) worry about ??

-(T)- -(U)- -(E)-

ie, rerun:

CRISS
-(T)- -(U)- -(X)-
CROSS

rerun
NOT ACCEPTABLE

And he's 000000 so good,

And he's 000000 so fine,

And he's 000000 so healthy

In his body and his mind:

The well respected man-about-town

Doin' the best things

soooc

con serv a tiv' ly

The Bottle

Have you ever witnessed an execution?
Have you ever witnessed an execution?
Have you ever witnessed an execution?
I Have.

There is really nothing to it.
There is really nothing to it.
There is really nothing to it.
Do You Hear Me?

I Said:

Have you ever witnessed an execution?
Have you ever witnessed an execution?
Have you ever witnessed an execution?
I Have.

There is really nothing to it.
There is really nothing to it.

There is only the situation   you are in   in that you are in the situation   only long enough   to witness the execution   of the situation   you are in

there is only the situation   of the execution   of the situation   of the execution   of the situation   of the execution you are in.

Have you held the bottle in your hands? Have you held it in your hands long enough to feel it? I Have. It is somewhat mysterious, the bottle, but it is not strange.

Yes, I have held and felt and seen the bottle thoroughly, held it in my hands, felt its makings in my heart, seen its colour, its shape, with my eyes. Have you held the bottle in your hands? I Have.

Actually, is there any man who, given the realitites of the situation, could have acted otherwise? Bruce certainly could not. He sighed. He could only turn the page.

Had he been able to do otherwise, he would certainly have done so. But the leaves followed the sun with the same ageless rhythm; the motions of Desire appeared to him briefly — then hid. He closed the book. It was the book of look. He had been reading the page of age. He pondered: 'There seems no 'proper' solution,' he thought. He pondered again. He pondered and pondered and pondered: 'Oh, there is no relief for me!' he sighed, and then he turned his head. True, the leaves DID still follow the sun in the same old way. Underneath his eyes, things were beginning to grow. He had to follow them too.

He got up and walked outside, tired of following the sun through the window inside. He followed the sun outside up the street to another place inside, inside where the room hid itself under the seat of Desire, only this time in a different form ...

He waited in the seat to be served the question to be answered by. This may appear confusing to the reader, or listener, yet do bear in mind that the actual *reality* of the situation was just as confusing to Bruce – perhaps more so; **HOWEVER**, in order to satisfy some of the minor aspects of detail pertaining to this confusion, we juxtapose upon the reader/listener the following scene:

Bruce had absconded to the nearby Telltale Bar on 64th Street, corner of Melon Square. There in the bliss of afternoons, he spent his Time. Not so much, again, for the meaning of it as for the loss of the meaning of it. The room was shabby, dull; lights blistered on the ceiling. Open sores poured from the eyes of customers long since gone into the dwellings of shadowland. In the corner sat Mr. Greeneyes. Mr. Cloak sat firmly in place as usual. All eyes turned on Bruce. Bruce turned on all eyes turned on him, but only for a moment or two.

NOW there was also in the Telltale Bar corner of Melon Square at that Time a barrister name of Slim Slantly, hailed from down Aberdeen way; sauntered up to Brucie and said: 'Listen chum, don't be so foolish get **OUT OUT OUT**.' '**HOW HOW HOW**?' Brucie replied. 'Never mind that now. Move over and let me sit down.' So he did and

'Brucie now,' he said, 'you told me last

week   to tell you this week   to tell you to tell me   to tell you to TELL ME TO TELL YOU TO TELL ME NOW NOW NOW and so I'm telling you *now*, telling you the way it is to tell.

and if you

cannot find it in your heart,   if you do not believe me now,   if you cannot find it in your heart   if you do not believe me now,   then I *shall* tell you, I *must* tell you   that I've told you, that I've just told you, just now; and this you must bear with you   over and above all other considerations   that it is as I have told you, that is, that it is NOW.'

Brucie shifted uncomfortably. He did not know immediately how to respond. 'Yes,' he said. 'I know.' He smiled. But he lied.

'Did you go to the races last night?' Slim asked him, changing the subject.

'Yes,' Brucie replied, watching Slim closely. For he did not know if Slim knew he had lied or not.

'How did you make out?'

'Lost $23.'

'Too bad.'

'Yoo.'

'And now?'

'Now?'

'What?'

'What?'

'Yes.'

'Well, I don't know,' Brucie sighed, trying again. 'You see, I can't seem to find the answer to the question of what I am looking for in this world, in this place, in this time, in this room here now.

I cannot find the answer to the question.

I cannot find the answer to the question.

I cannot find the answer to the question.

Do You Hear Me?'

'Yes I hear you,' Slim replied.
'Yes I hear you,' Slim replied.
'Yes I hear you.' But he lied.

'There was this bottle, see,' Brucie went on. 'I held it, see, I felt it moving, saw it, held it saw it felt it ... the reality of the bottle in investigating its possibilities came across in the leaves following the sun ... in through the bottle the leaves ... in through the bottle following picked up the sun ... first only a thread of light, a strand but I SAW IT I know I saw it. I know I did.

'SAW IT AS the witness saw the execution as the child saw the bottle as the adult saw the leaves following the sun following the child for the first, the very first, time.

I took the bottle in my hands,' he said. 'You won't believe me if I tell you. I saw *the same thing* in the bottle as Isaw in the leaves, the sun, the child: each of them following each other around. Each of them following each other around.'

Slantly laughed. 'You expect me to believe that?'

'Believe what you like. I will not try to convince you. I felt the trembling of the bottle in my hand. I saw it begin to glow, at first bluish-white, then a deep blue; the trembling, the glow increased beyond me, until I could no longer feel it or see it. After a time, the trembling subsided, the blueness began to fade, and the bottle was gone.

'Where had it gone? I cannot find the answer to the question. It had gone to the leaves, to the sun, to the child who witnessed the execution. How did it go? Here is the question we wait to be answered by.

'I have tried to tell you this and you have said that you would tell me if it were true. I have listened to you trying to tell me so, but I can't believe you: in fact I lied when I said that I did believe you, just before you changed the subject.

'Whether or not you believe me now, I don't know.'

'Now as it happens I must close the door and continue. The saga of the bottle is over. Believe it or not as you will, Slantly. I don't know whether to believe it myself.'

Downtown

Go where we all go
When we're feeling ever so low,
When we're feeling lonely & down,
When all we do is frown

ha ha

Go to where the action is:

D
D T
Do To
Dow Tow
Down Town

G GG   G GG
oGoo   oGoo
o   o
own   own
Down   Town
own   own

own   own
Down   Town
own   own
o   o
oGoo   oGoo
G GG   G GG

"How're things therrrrrrrrrrrrrrrrrre...

at the office today?"

"What'll it be sir?"

"Ex."

ppphhhizzzzzzz

RING IN

$000000000000000000000000000000000000000000000000000000000000000000000000000000000.90 - B
click
click
click
$000000000000000000000000000000000000000000000000000000000000000000000000000000000.90 - TL B

THANK YOU

again
again
again

"whereIworky'meanwhereImakemylikelivelihoodincome?"

"Incidentally, why do you wear a cross?"

"I'm a C.. a C.. a C.. a CCC..Christian, but I can't see where it's any of

<u>your</u> damn business."

 h r
w e e ffffffriendly people
 e r
w a a ffffff

riendly smile

"No, but seriously, have you seen him?"

"No, not tonight. Why? Who is he? Why are you so anxious to see him?"

"He's my friend."

"_I_ don't know him."

dat dat, da-dish di   a   a h   n n d o a h y
Wedi dit dit dot da da   a h   n n d o a h y
Welldit dot dit dit da da h   n n d o a h y
Well, dit di-da da dish dah   n n d o a h y
Well, I dot didoddit da do don n d o a h y
Well, I bedan di da da do do don d o a h y
Well, I bet di-do done do-do day d o a h y
Well, I bet myda-do, da-do, doo dooo a h y
Well, I bet my Mdo-da, do-da, daa daaa h y
Well, I bet my MONdah-do, dah-do, dahhhh y
Well, I bet my MONEYdo-day, do-dah dayyyyy

$
---$37.79---

---$24.95--a-saving-fo

stock (inventory clear away!)

---$17.99--a-sav

winter

spring $ $ $

special

$ SALE!! I N T R I C $ $ $

SALE!! $

overload $ COLLULOID FABRICATE

$

fall

summer   . textured constacrese cloth $ $

company

$ $. never needs ironing (interweave) $

TUDOR   780   SEDAN : $

DODGE   . won't: shrink, fade, wrinkle, frazzle,

T   U - $ $. insured against fire, all the modern

Company car, low mileage V-8 engine,   death, water,

TONE   automatic transmission, push button radio, power steering,

O
V

SAVE
New Price: $3898   S A V E   SAVEEEEYYYYOUUUSSSAVE
SALE Price: $[illegible]579   SAVE

R
$
$
$

$$$$$$$$$$$$$$$$$$$$$one thousand
three hundreds

wwwwwwwwwwhhhhhhhhhhwhwhwhwhwhwhwhwhrrrrrrrrrOOOOOOMM: R -/‾ 2 1
P -/_ 3

"Veddy noooiiiice day, tobesure. I say

ol' chappie,
bosom bud,
dearest friend,
constant comrade,

I say

l o o k

at the poor zouls 'o 'ave to walk 'ome; 'o 'ave to get on those

dirty trolleys."

GO

wwwwwwwwwwhhhhhhhhhhwhwhwhwhwhwhwhwhrrrrrrrrrOOOOOOMM:

```
        I N S E R T   C O I N

        turn handle to right
        as  far  as possible
        after each coin


        9:30 AM  to  4:30 PM

    0    6    12    18    24    30
    //////////////////////////////
                 s
                t t
               o   o
              p G O p
               o   o
                t t
                 s
    //////////////////////////////
       36    42    48    54    60

        MONDAY   -   FRIDAY
```

"How are you tonight sir?"

"Not bad. I'll have the ch- the ch- the chicken stew."

"Mashed or french fries?"

"M-Mashed."

"Soup or juice?"

"S-Soup or juice?"

T Y
h COMMERCIAL
a RESTAURANT o
n
Yonge at k Y u Toronto P
Gerrard
F o r a

/ chick st u t $1.40

r tax -

o
no 4041 Guests Waiter
n / 7

a
PLEASE PAY
g $1.40
CASHIER
e

"Do you want to tell me about it?"

"No. No, not right now."

"Can you make it next Tuesday?"

"Same time?"

"Same time."

"Good evening sir. My name is (shake hands) Jim Sloane.
I'm getting some opinions on a new nation-wide programme in the field of educational p
however I am required to speak to both you and your wife.
Is she in?"

a) "Yes."
"Do you mind if
I step in?"

b) "I'm busy."
"That's all right sir,
it'll just take a few
moments of your time."

c) "Not interested."
"That's understandable
sir, however, it doesnt
require any interest."

d) "What are
"Oh, perh
me correc
some opin

"However, as I said, I am required to speak to both you and your wi

Is she in?

"One please."

just one

M T W E N
6 C E N
8 T H E A
5 a d m i
3 $1.

"Thank you."

so much

again
again

"Wouldn't ya liketa have that eh? EH? EH? Gimme a smoke."

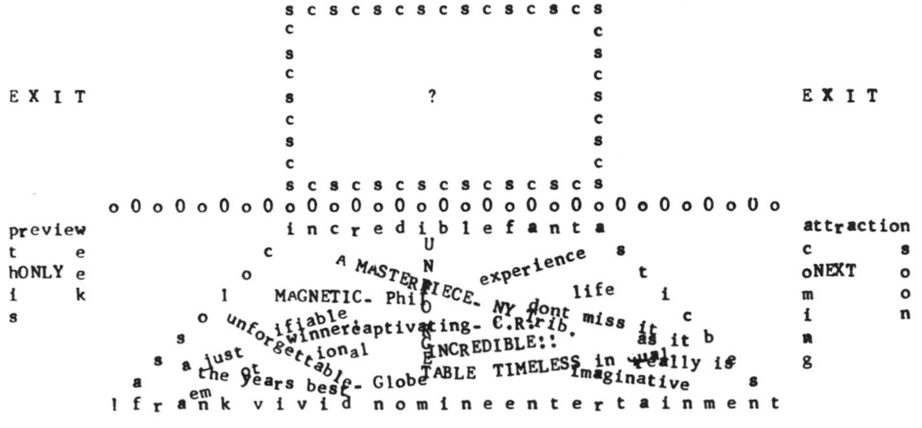
EXIT
?
EXIT
incrediblefanta
preview
attraction
ONLY
NEXT
coming
soon
A MASTERPIECE- NY
experience
MAGNETIC- Phil
life
dont miss it
unforgettable
winnercaptivating- C.R.rib.
INCREDIBLE!!
as it really is
TABLE TIMELESS
Imaginative
the years best- Globe
frank vivid nomineentertainment

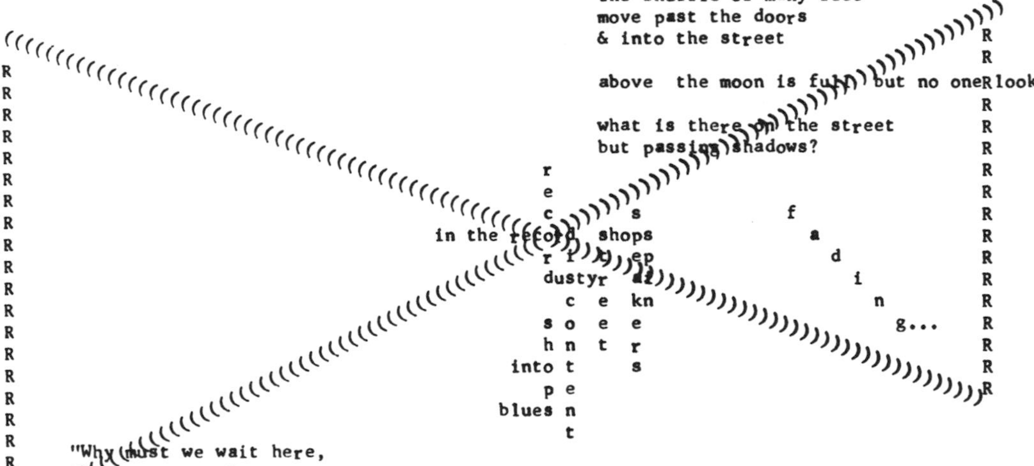
the shuffle of many feet
move past the doors
& into the street
above the moon is full but no one looks
what is there on the street
but passing shadows?
in the record shops
dusty
into
blues
f a d i n g...
"Why must we wait here,
Can't we go on?
I don't understand dear,
The beat of the song."

● 0 o 0 o 0 o 0 o 0 o 0 o
0 0
o TTNNOGOTWWGGGGODDDOND o
0 OTGONNTWWGGGGOONODDDO 0
o WTNNOGOTOOGGGGWWDDNOW o
0 NTOGONNTWTGGGGOONODDN 0
o NTNNOGOTWWGGGGOODDDDN o
0 0
o 0 o 0 o 0 o 0 o 0 o 0 o

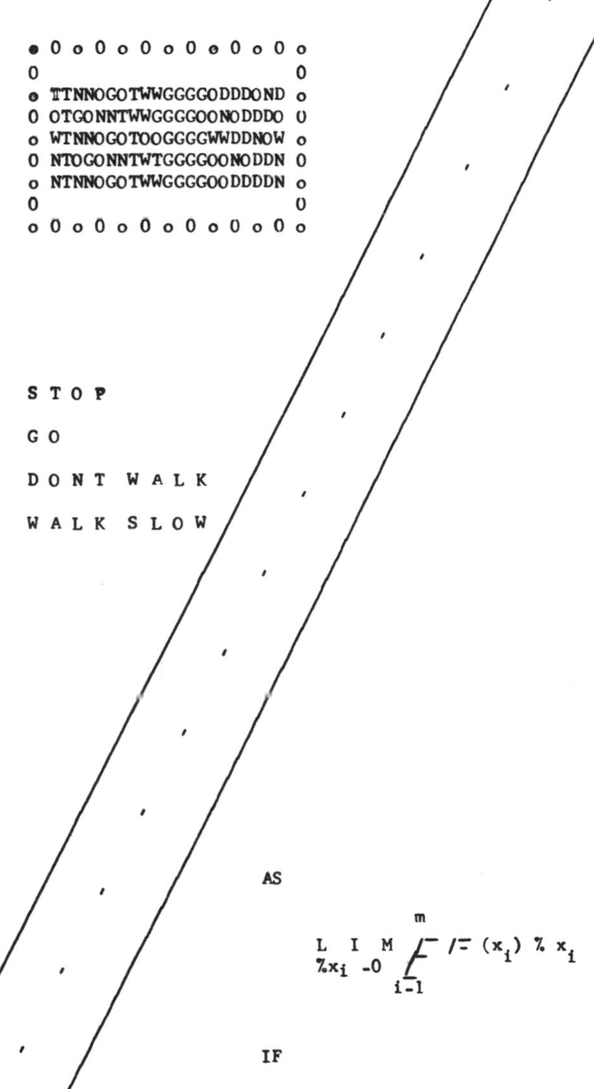

S T O P

G O

D O N T W A L K

W A L K S L O W

AS

$$\underset{\% x_i\ -0}{\mathrm{L\;\;I\;\;M}} \sum_{i-1}^{m} /= (x_i)\ \%\ x_i$$

IF

0

o

0000000
00000
00

Home again, 0 o o

0 o

One lies in bed o 0 o 0

0 o 0 o

Smsmsmsmsmsmsmsm:::.

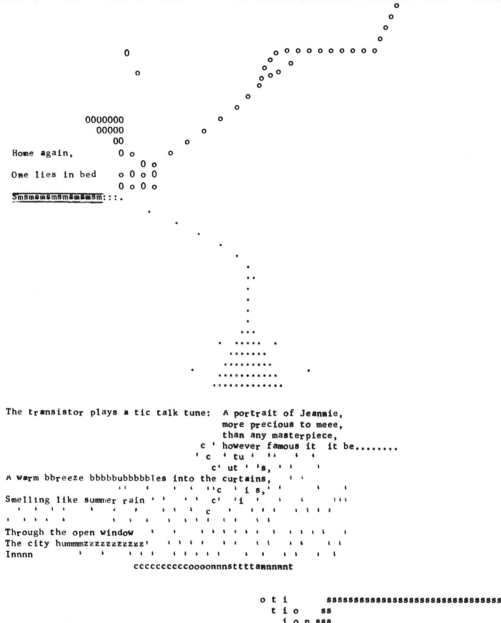

The transistor plays a tic talk tune: A portrait of Jeannie,
more precious to meee,
than any masterpiece,
c ' however famous it it be........
' c ' tu
c' ut ' 's,
A warm bbreeze bbbbbubbbbbles into the curtains,
''c ' i s,'
Smelling like summer rain c' 'i
c
Through the open window
The city hummmzzzzzzzzzzz'
Innnn
cccccccccccoooonnnsttttannnant

o t i sssssssssssssssssssssssssssssssss
t i o ss
i o n sss
'mmmmmmmmmmsssssssssssssssssssssssssssssssss
o t i sss
t i o ss
i o n sssssssssssssssssssssssssssssssss

Break

-on th porch most uv th day. dont evin go intu
town now no more   why smell fer th same
aye sits by th door on th porch most uv th day   doesnt
go intu town now dark thots in his dark head who knows whut
his brother thinks
ust tu think arnold was th crazy one member he usd tu wander
round high all th time quoting frum classicul literature diaries & all
tried tu cut off his ear onct jacob stopped him
now probably wouldnt give a damn ill bet hed evein hand him th knife

soo we goo frum there tu here   jacob in th back
yard howin corn feedin th chickins is thinking bout th clumps
of earth & cobbles
his brain rattles slightly as he luks skyward
well sumbodys
got tu tell whut happind
luks skyward & begins tu see

the arc lay
perpenDicular
to the plaNe
agaInst thE
table wHere
we sat
no it was never meant that way he sD tho it may have seemed so

it is a running game you are playing she replied.

arnold
is rocking back & forth there is an old oak tree must have a trunk 6·
acrost in the middle uv th front yard casts shade everywhere never cud
cut it down th
raises

& shouts 'no its no good leave it alone!'

monday 3pm. open th door & noone there. rises to greet his lady friend
Isobel. Isobel is an alcoholic lives down by th tracks with sum friends
drinks herself silly by th cobblestones all day gets high/as trains go by
feed th sun yellow germ we turn we think we do she is as many as is a
single she femininity
soft heather with no-name we call you remember this kiss a feeling for us
as well stall stell shill arraignge.
those same afternoon we usd to walk down that way & observe them all all
crazy th lot uv them. the whole family littul wonder someday one uv them
jacob i think blew th barn down & galloped on outahere. w tu th big city never
caught him neither. sumday mebbe expect one of them sumone sez mebbe cum back
cum back cum back

& littul arnold he didnt evin
bat an eye just sat there
on th front porch

watch him ride out & th barn fall down & thot 'figures' tho nobody really knows

yeah yeah found him there sitting there one day later soon think it was jeb th marshall 1st thing he noticed th clothes seemed awful loose hey arnie he says yer clothes seem but then th spell wore off n e got closer too saw just th skeleton left, clothes old worn died right ther th birds pickd him clean laid an egg right by his door

s w
o ejawin with yew
L
F 1
a s
r
b
s i
bUt i got to go Now anyway

f n
O i a
r c g
yew iD seen thIs is a place & beeN Gone but
i
when this you hear then i am near

so jacob lkd bt th old place grass growin over everythin evin his ears now how as i reckon he thot but th dust blew that one over too could cind uv get to like it here he thot if only th still of only th words will if only this fit place cud be mine for th asking tu keeping it free frum all th birds eyed his dearly beloved still sitting there propped up against th porch (jeb nailed his shirt tu th woodwork) oops an arm fell off well arnie thot that is frst things theys got tu go

guesS so
Into

The sky a cloud
l o
o w
u n
dRops

thru thE foliaGe

reVealing a loNg tubU laR
structurE

eX Ist I NgEver
thru thE veil oF careS
so carefully knoWn
'well wEll shall we' he replIed
Th En
'I say
Go?'

clouD
Drops
stariNg
hEavily

Down

transpontine schizophyceous yeuk unguiculate skink
quinqueremes choledochotomy gaberlunzie xanthochroid
jactitation bifid poltroonery trismegistus diopter
foudroyant achech misericord hemerasia gaberlunzie
gyttja viscerotropism nauplius dysarthria quincunx
chlorotrifluoromethane yataghan katabatic urticaceous
phthisic exonarthex mazegane zygapophysis inquinal
sarraceniaceous wrouskian jequirity zischagge qutb
scherzando gree galvanoplasty pseudepigrapha varix
chordatendinea svarabhakti hyperprosexia leptorrhiny
yttrotantalite pervicacious yggdrasil eath pantoum
urtication rawinsonde nystagmus zanthoxylum oology
orthotoluidine saxifrage fainaigne laurustinus zif

scuse me what am i doing here... no well we might cum sure i
mean im mean good night for it dance after all these years & th barn rebuilt
never could
figgure out what happind then
who was she or evin who passed thru

kind uv kill those old dust bowls & evin now when i go
huntin i take leo with me hes a new boy in town but maryjane
is th sweetest fillie ever grazed a pasture
we all gathered
arnold sumwhere out brooding (we didnt know it wuz
happening) then th whol damn thing falls in seems he had it rigged right
frum th start with chains & nellybelle & ralph th steer steered her
straight intu perdition u askd me i mean she finally did roast anyway tough old
bird tho when she got too old to fuck
well th lanterns caught th hay n th barn wuz gone in no time
i found
him laughin hisself silly in th valley his favourite place & pretty near kilt
him i guess i damaged his skull or sumthin th doctors seys hasint bin th same
since just sits & glowers on th porch most uv th day thinks to himself 'figures'
tho noone knows for sure
well so thats th time uv it peers he was in
love with maryjane hisself but couldnt do it but fer sum crazy actions! ha! they
thot _i_ wuz crazy well meet th champ!

dad? he run off with Isobel the alkie down by th river th tracks cum
uppin & onct one day they both board a cattle car headid east & thet wuz
all jeb passed by old daddy yells out tu him SHOVE IT JEB JUST FUCKIN WELL
SHOVE IT laughs hisself silly & falls down always kinda likta think mebbe
he got roasted with th rest uv them critters/tho likely hed be too tough too.

but listen dont want to strain yer ear none mister
by th way whut u doin here anyway? never did tell me yer
business.'i cum tu pay th price' he sez weirdest critter i ever seen
then walks off intu a clouda dust & disappears mebbe hes a vampire or sumthin

tHe LOOK OvEr In HIS hAnDs ThE

mushrooms soft crunch under

ThE dElIcAtE tOuCh Of HiS tEeTh

we have come a long way since then..

arc descending slowly into the horizontal infinite
at the last moment takes a turn to the east
dissolving slowly in a ray of sun.
she had committed suicide when i last saw her.
(however not in the def 'in it ive sense')
there are many paths to take to avoid
many paths to take

well
we kin all tolerate
tu a certain length
trubble if yew
know whut i mean   mister
eh if yew know whut i mean mister
                                    well
mother crazy arnold strangled
her in th crib   littul wonder
she cud hardly bring him up
properly i dont know whether
  is anybody knows about her

so anyways after the
examination of the
fragmentation is whut i think
led personally tu th breakdown
till after a while yew
couldnt tell yew
follow me mister after a while yew

   whut yew say yer name was? frum where?
so he carried on after lengthy considerations (sigh!) ah
it wuz a great time of life fer me mister let me tell yew! a great time!
   well after jacob left & they put arnold away i got maryjane
lock stock & cock worked for a time down at laebs store in town/
got to know everybody eh sit around gossip all day drink beer yew get
the picture hot sun black flies lot uv drinkin cussin & pissin well we
left our valuables behind long ago son long ago

   whut line uv work yew say yew in?
then th bookeepers & th lumber crew for th edge uv th forest cum & tuk
it all away o i dont know sum paper company up north no nothin ull
happin they sd nothin ull happin lull yew tu sleep while they rob yew
blind & th pocketbook gone tew well i stayed on fer awhile then threw
it all in. whut was th use? th land gone the wind dried up th village
bell didnt give a damn any more, no, not anymore no not no way. oh well

   thot id throw that in
   'what dew yew mean' th stranger sd taking off
his hat thumpin it against his thighs the dust rose
been on a long trip mister looks like you been in the saddle a long time
i mean look at that dust
   'what dew yew mean' th stranger sd whut
dew yew mean i askd him but then
 he did the strangest thing
  got up & walked away
 a dustcloud swallered him   only a few seconds just as tho he wasnt there
horse & all   just up & disappeared mebbe
         hes a vampire or sumthin

he strolled boldly across the lawn/sat down
   sun shifting thru a few leaves/blossoms gathering somewhere in a corner
      concave curve shifting slowly onto a lateral plane
         (imagined flattened as a vertical rise)
            revolving slowly ever so slowly
               we had mapped before (mid-right-hand grid
                 compass lost
                  travelling on an incertainty
                  (hoping for) (words)(fuel)(the best)
                 imprints in the sand/pecker tracks
               leaf thru ordinary conversations
            words dipped in too easily
         shape honey-lights moths die from burning out
      glue-formations adhereing to the skin one is caught
   too easily as a fly on a leaf of sticky paper dangling
in the air for anyone to chew

amending securing us perpendicular to the central view
accosted approximately zen degrees north south ideologically we spin

used to walk by th back a
th old mill western edge
a town when old man miller
lived there shootin
out his windows fuckin
his pimple-faced daughter with
that body out of th next
century

one day pickd up a gun
member that blew
his head off

jeff **chuckled. yeah** them were th **days.**
& you knew if we had to do them over again
would we do them over again
or get shot ourselves
halfway thru or mebbe evin git
abortid

well jeff yes jeff sure jeff
i always wondered about that jeff
boy you was a good shot
when you was young.

"to the north we follow the trail without sense   leave our
decisions behind   sand building up on our feet   we turn
at the horizon merge the vertical accidentally bumps into
us what is it she says nothing i say nothing it is a shape
of some sort (being unable to define a grid connection) some
passing conjunctive phase... i suggested

fortunately the temperature here drops at night.
we dream a lot in the winter."

30000 Please control tower!
come in! come in! we aRe in trouble!
is perpendicular figured 30000 feet crOssing the desert
aCtion emerges
horizontal backdrop sprEads her legs
vertical incision Steadily erect
"kinda makeS yew think
mebbe therll be
mOre weather when we need it"
iF

grid line becomes the phantom Imagination we are witness to
ceNtral
Control speaking... move to the left please
thank you vast aReas spilling thru skies revivisectifying
20000 (somewherE the moon bursts)
i dunno nohow he nodded his head uncertAinly dont know
lookS up at the sky never see enuff of it
wow its like a fallIng star eh
passing grid coordiNates right ascension 7 hours 8 minutes
declination 24 deGrees 3 days past summer solstice
overlay of clouds
undeRlay of rain
flAttened axial
inTerlock
imposed upon a centrIfugal pattern
peels an Orange thinks mebbe hes right peels fall
off his orange onto his lap off his lap oNto the floor are
swept up sumtyme out into the yArd
why shouLd she/
10000 she muttered bElow
as the plane flew unseen
overhead whut is that? shE sd i dont know likely
some sort of conjunctiVe phase...
how long we bin herE now who gives a shit go shut th godamned
door all the flies are gettiN in & YOU you jerk!
some interaction of particles as assembLes any entity given we have been given so much
to destroY
5000
whut wuz that? hell jacob hell i sD "lets go take a look"
"hell no" he sd all theyll remember us for Is our balls
not our boneS
cmon jacob cmon at leasT assume the pose-
diRt
stIll
Beam
dUsty
flaT
thE
winDows
along the floor where we sit sipping tea

The Space Where Love Should Be

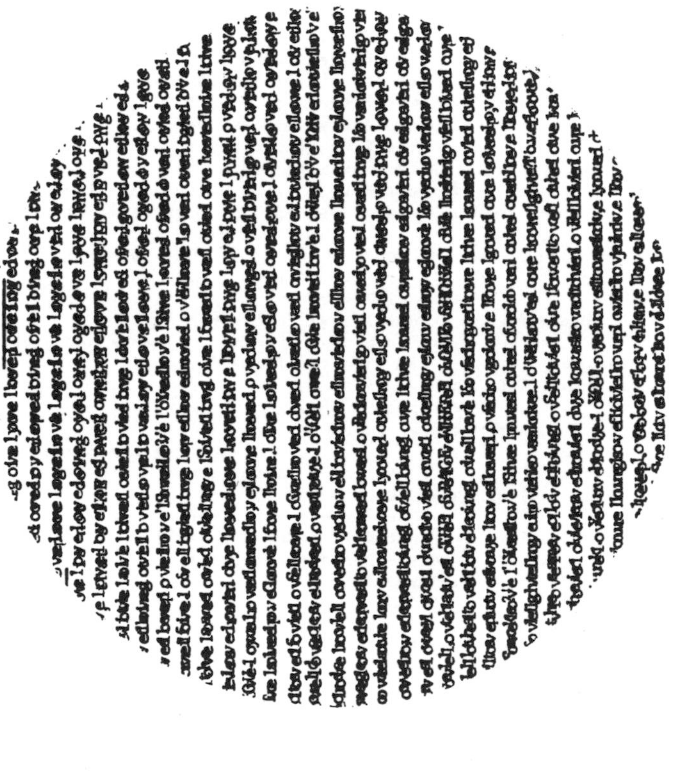

velovelovelovelovelove
lovelovelovelovelove
elovelovelovelovelove
elovelovelovelovelove
velovelovelovelovelove
elovelovelovelovelove
velovelovelovelovelove
elovelovelovelovelove
velovelovelovelovelove
velovelovelovelove
ovelovelovelovelove
ovelovelovelovelove
ovelovelovleovelove
ovelovelovelovelove
lovelovelovelovelove
ovelovelovelovelove
lovelovelovelovelove
ovelovelovelovelove
lovelovelovelovelove
velovelovelovelove
ovelovelovelovelove
ovelovelovelovelove
ovelovelovelovelove
ovelovelovelovelove
ovelovelovelovelove
velovelovelovelove
velovelovelovelove
ovelovelovelovelove
elovelovelovelove
lovelovelovelove
velovelovelove
ovelovelove

ght without love. &
goes under, empty. "Oh me?
Why?" "Oh nothin'." Words rol
ns inside. The moon haunts y
yes. Boozing it away tv ea
r whatever your thing is
quer, repeating filling
in in a way you know
wrong, well, that's
d up with all that sh
thing till its put aw
"Smoke?" "Yeah." S
ting up the smoke.
thing. Sittin in fror
e nothin'. Filling
our head, your lun
him. To sleep. So it
in to bed late at
"Oh me? Oh nothin
ns inside. The m
Boozing it away
r your thing is
ing filling up t
you know is r
g, well, that's
filled up wi
otten the sam
sleep, for
moke?" "Yeah
e table. T

the same
. Sittin in front of
v watchin their lives drain by
chin. Fillin up with junk. Your body-
U- your stomach, your head, your lungs- f
with junk. To sleep. Good for him. To sleep.
it starts. Like to sleep. Lots of it. Sleep. Goi
bed late at night without love. & the world goes un
npty. "Oh me? Oh nothin'. Why?" "Oh nothin'." Words rol
ver you. Visions inside. The moon haunts your brain. Imag
peat themselves. Boozing it away tv eating & smoking it to
eath, or whatever your thing is you keep doing over & over
ver, repeating filling up the same space again & again & agai
n a way you know is not doing you any good & you know is wrong
ell, that's THE SPACE WHERE LOVE SHOULD BE being filled up wit
ll that shit being dulled & forgotten the same old thing till
put away to sleep, for good. Sleep, him. "Smoke?"
he puts food on the table. lighting up the smoke.
n tonight?" in front of th
v watchin Fillin up with
junk. Your lungs- f
up with start

LOVE SHOULD BE

eing filled up with all th

t being dulled & forgotten the sa

d thing till its put away to sleep, for

od. For good to sleep, him. "Smoke?" "Yeah."

ue puts food on the table. Terrific. & lighting

ne smoke. "What's on tonight?"-- food & the same o

ing. Sittin in front of the tv watchin their lives dr

because nothin. Fillin up with junk. Your body YOU

our stomach, your head, your lungs- fillin up with junk.

eep. Good for him, to sleep. So it starts. Life to sleep.

s of it. Sleep. Goin to bed late at night without love. & the

orld goes under, empty. "Oh me? Oh nothin', why?" "Oh nothin'.

ords roll over you. Visions inside. The moon haunts your brain.

mages repeat themselves. Boozing it away tv eating & smoking it

o death, or whatever your thing is you keep doing it over & ove

over, repeating filling up the same space again & again & agai

n a way you know is not doing you any good & you know is wrong.

vell, that's THE SPACE WHERE LOVE SHOULD BE being filled up wi

ll that shit being dulled & forgotten the same old thing

ts put away to sleep, for good. For good to sleep, him.

"Yeah." She puts food on the table. Terrific. &

smoke. "What's on tonight?"-- food & the same

in front of the tv watchin their lives drain

nothin. Fillin up with junk. Your body, YOU

our head, your lungs- fillin up with junk.

Good for him, to sleep. So it starts

Lots of it. Sleep. Goin to bed late

ithout love. & the world goes under

"Oh me? Oh nothin'. Why?" "Oh nothin'."

ords roll over you. Visions

moon haunts your

lovelovelovelovelove

lovelovelovelovelovelovelove

lovelovelovelovelovelovelovelovelove

lovelovelovelovelovelovelovelovelovelove

lovelovelovelovelovelovelovelovelovelovelove

lovelovelovelovelovelovelovelovelovelovelovelove

lovelovelovelovelovelovelovelovelovelovelovelove

lovelovelovelovelovelovelovelovelovelovelovelove

lovelovelovelovelovelovelovelovelovelovelovelove

lovelovelovelovelovelovelovelovelovelovelovelove

lovelovelovelovelovelovelovelovelovelovelove

lovelovelovelovelovelovelovelovelovelove

lovelovelovelovelovelovelovelovelove

lovelovelovelovelovelovelove

lovelovelovelovelove

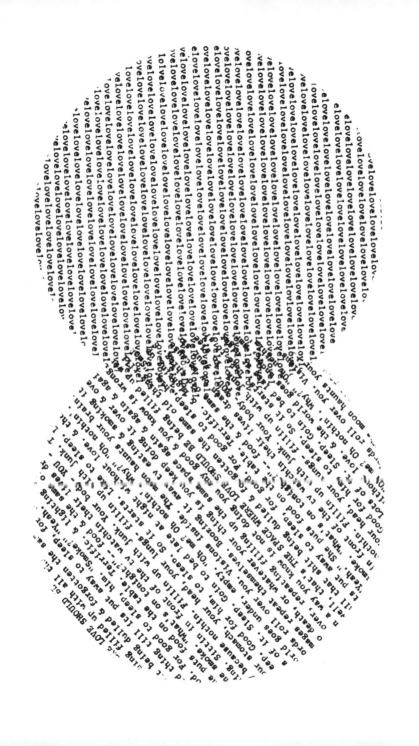

[illegible]
ozing it away tv eat[illegible]
oking it to death, or whatever
ng is you keep doing over & over & o[illegible]
eating filling up the same space again &
gain in a way you know is not doing you any go
you know is wrong, well, that's THE SPACE WHERE
OVE SHOULD BE being filled up with all that shit be
led & forgotten the same old thing till its all put aw
sleep, for good. For good to sleep, him. "Smoke?" "Yeah
e put the food on the table. Terrific. & lighting up the s
hat's on tonight?"-- food & the same old thing. Sittin in f
the tv watchin their lives drain by because nothin'. Fillin
th junk. Your body- YOU- your stomach, your head, your lungs
llin up with junk. To sleep. Good for him, to sleep. So it st
e to sleep. Lots of it. Sleep. Goin to bed late at night with
e. & the world goes under, empty. "Oh me? Oh nothin'. Why?" "
thin'." Filled with fear she turned away. Why was she afraid?
e did not know; &, she thot, 'it may well happen again...' &
ere it was, pounding along the surface of THE SBACE WHERE LO
HOULD BE, sewing that space up tight with (in her case) fear
hough it could as well have been anything, anything 'to hav
t all,' as she thot, 'happen again.' Something filling in
a substitute from which there was no escape into the lov
ehind it all; & so, the circle begins again. He dreamt
he was eating fruit from a bowl. It was delicious. S
guard came & took him to jail. He locked him in
ell & said: "You will be executed shortly." Th
clouds were low. He used a large hook to la
nto one of them, & rose up higher & h
into the air. It grew unbearably c
He woke in the darkness of
oom. listening t[illegible]

lovelovelove
lovelovelovelovelovelo
ovelovelovelovelovelovelovelo
velovelovelovelovelovelovelovelove
ovelovelovelovelovelovelovelovelovelov
elovelovelovelovelovelovelovelovelovelovel
elovelovelovelovelovelovelovelovelovelovelove
ovelovelovelovelovelovelovelovelovelovelovelovel
ovelovelovelovelovelovelovelovelovelovelovelovelov
velovelovelovelovelovelovelovelovelovelovelovelovelo
velovelovelovelovelovelovelovelovelovelovelovelovelove
velovelovelovelovelovelovelovelovelovelovelovelovelovel
ovelovelovelovelovelovelovelovelovelovelovelovelovelovel
ovelovelovelovelovelovelovelovelovelovelovelovelovelovelo
lovelovelovelovelovelovelovelovelovelovelovelovelovelovelo
velovelovelovelovelovelovelovelovelovelovelovelovelovelove
lovelovelovelovelovelovelovelovelovelovelovelovelovelovelo
velovelovelovelovelovelovelovelovelovelovelovelovelovelove
lovelovelovelovelovelovelovelovelovelovelovelovelovelovelo
ovelovelovelovelovelovelovelovelovelovelovelovelovelovelov
elovelovelovelovelovelovelovelovelovelovelovelovelovelov
velovelovelovelovelovelovelovelovelovelovelovelovelovel
velovelovelovelovelovelovelovelovelovelovelovelovelove
elovelovelovelovelovelovelovelovelovelovelovelovelov
ovelovelovelovelovelovelovelovelovelovelovelovelov
elovelovelovelovelovelovelovelovelovelovelovelov
ovelovelovelovelovelovelovelovelovelovelovel
elovelovelovelovelovelovelovelovelovelove
elovelovelovelovelovelovelovelovelove
velovelovelovelovelovelovelovelovel
lovelovelovelovelovelovelovel
ovelovelovelovelovelovel

at the silence, s...
by the wall, awake, disturb...
visions inside. The dream. Words roll over you.
Images repeat themselves. The moon haunts your bra...
smoking it to death, or whatever. Boozing it away tv ...
p doing over & over & over, repeating your thing is ...
same space again & again & again in a way filling up
doing you any good & you know is wrong, well, you know
WHERE LOVE SHOULD BE being filled up with all tha...
ed & forgotten the same old thing till its all that ...
or good. For good to sleep, him. "Smoke?" put away
e table. Terrific. & lighting up the smoke. "Yeah." S
food & the same old thing. Sittin in front of "What"...
lives drain by because nothin. Fillin up with the t...
tomach, your head, your lungs- fillin up with junk
eep. So it starts. Like to sleep. Lots of it. Sle...
ight without love. & the world goes under, empty
, "Oh nothin'." Words roll over you. Visions ins...
rain. Images repeat themselves. Filled with fea...
was she afraid? She did not know; &, she thot
..' & there it was, pounding along the surfa...
LOVE SHOULD BE, sewing that space up tight
ear, though it could as well have been an
hot, 'happen again.' Something filling
h there was no escape into the loving
, the circle begins again. Boozing ...
g & smoking it to death, or what...
is you keep doing over & over & ...
ng filling up the same spac...
& again & again in a wa...
know is not doing ...

velovelovelovelovelovelovelovelov
ovelovelovelovelovelovelovelovelo.
velovelovelovelovelovelovelovelovelo.
ovelovelovelovelovelovelovelovelovelove
velovelovelovelovelovelovelovelovelovelo.
velovelovelovelovelovelovelovelovelovelo
velovelovelovelovelovelovelovelovelovelove
velovelovelovelovelovelovelovelovelovelovelo
ovelovelovelovelovelovelovelovelovelovelove
ovelovelovelovelovelovelovelovelovelovelovel
elovelovelovelovelovelovelovelovelovelovelovel
ovelovelovelovelovelovelovelovelovelovelovelov
elovelovelovelovelovelovelovelovelovelovelovel
velovelovelovelovelovelovelovelovelovelovelove
velovelovelovelovelovelovelovelovelovelovelovelo
lovelovelovelovelovelovelovelovelovelovelovelove
velovelovelovelovelovelovelovelovelovelovelovelo
lovelovelovelovelovelovelovelovelovelovelovelove
velovelovelovelovelovelovelovelovelovelovelovelo
lovelovelovelovelovelovelovelovelovelovelovelo
ovelovelovelovelovelovelovelovelovelovelov
elovelovelovelovelovelovelovelovelovelov
ovelovelovelovelovelovelovelovelovelovel
elovelovelovelovelovelovelovelovelovelove
velovelovelovelovelovelovelovelovelove
velovelovelovelovelovelovelovelovelov
velovelovelovelovelovelovelovelovelo
velovelovelovelovelovelovelovelovelo
lovelovelovelovelovelovelovelovelo
ovelovelovelovelovelovelove
lovelovelovelovelovelov

lovelove
lovelovelovelovelove
velovelovelovelovelovelovelove
elovelovelovelovelovelovelovelove
ovelovelovelovelovelovelovelovelove
elovelovelovelovelovelovelovelovelove
velovelovelovelovelovelovelovelovelovelov
ovelovelovelovelovelovelovelovelovelovelovel
ovelovelovelovelovelovelovelovelovelovelove
ovelovelovelovelovelovelovelovelovelovelovelo
ovelovelovelovelovelovelovelovelovelovelovelove
ovelovelovelovelovelovelovelovelovelovelovelovelo
velovelovelovelovelovelovelovelovelovelovelovelov
elovelovelovelovelovelovelovelovelovelovelovelove
ovelovelovelovelovelovelovelovelovelovelovlvoelovelove
ovelovelovelovelovelovelovelovelovelovelovelovelove
velovelovelovelovelovelovelovelovelovelovelovelovel
elovelovelovelovelovelovelovelovelovelovelovelovelo
velovelovelovelovelovelovelovelovelovelovelovelovel
velovelovelovelovelovelovelovelovelovelovelovelov
elovelovelovelovelovelovelovelovelovelovelovelove
velovelovelovelovelovelovelovelovelovelovelovel
velovelovelovelovelovelovelovelovelovelovelove
velovelovelovelovelovelovelovelovelovelovelovelo
lovelovelovelovelovelovelovelovelovelovelovelo
vlovelovelovelovelovelovelovelovelovelovelo
velovelovelovelovelovelovelovelovelovelov
elovelovelovelovelovelovelovelovelovelo
velovelovelovelovelovelovelovelovelovelo
lovelovelovelovelovelovelovelovelovel
ovelovelovelovelovelovelovelove
elovelovelovelovelovelovelove
velovelovelovelovelo

know is
that's THE SPACE WHE
SHOULD BE being filled up wi
at shit being dulled & forgotten the
d thing till its all put away to slee
d. For good to sleep, him. "Smoke?" "
e put food on the table. Terrific. &
hat's on tonight?"-- food & the same
eir lives drain by because nothin'.
dy- YOU - your stomach, your head,
nk. To sleep. Good for him, to slee
o sleep. Lots of it. Sleep. Goin t
der, empty. He dreamt he was eat
Suddenly a guard came & took hi
louds were low. He used a lar
igher & higher into the air.
darkness, listening to the "O
isturbed by the dream.
othin'." Words roll ov
hemselves. Boozing
r whatever your th
over, repeating
again & again
doing you a
well, tha
illed

lovelove
elovelovelovelovelovelov
elovelovelovelovelovelovelovelov
elovelovelovelovelovelovelovelovel
elovelovelovelovelovelovelovelovelovel
elovelovelovelovelovelovelovelovelovelovel
velovelovelovelovelovelovelovelovelovelovelove
lovelovelovelovelovelovelovelovelovelovelovelove
velovelovelovelovelovelovelovelovelovelovelovelovel
elovelovelovelovelovelovelovelovelovelovelovelovel
ovelovelovelovelovelovelovelovelovelovelovelovelovel
lovelovelovelovelovelovelovelovelovelovelovelovelove
ovelovelovelovelovelovelovelovelovelovelovelovelovelov
lovelovelovelovelovelovelovelovelovelovelovelovelovelo
velovelovelovelovelovelovelovelovelovelovelovelovelovel
lovelovelovelovelovelovelovelovelovelovelovelovelovelove
velovelovelovelovelovelovelovelovelovelovelovelovelovel
lovelovelovelovelovelovelovelovelovelovelovelovelovelove
elovelovelovelovelovelovelovelovelovelovelovelovelovel
lovelovelovelovelovelovelovelovelovelovelovelovelovel
velovelovelovelovelovelovelovelovelovelovelovelovelo
ovelovelovelovelovelovelovelovelovelovelovelovelove
lovelovelovelovelovelovelovelovelovelovelovelovel
velovelovelovelovelovelovelovelovelovelovelovel
lovelovelovelovelovelovelovelovelovelovelovel
lovelovelovelovelovelovelovelovelovelovelovelo
elovelovelovelovelovelovelovelovelovelovelov
ovelovelovelovelovelovelovelovelovelovelo
velovelovelovelovelovelovelovelovelo
ovelovelovelovelovelovelovelovel
lovelovelovelovelovelovelovel
ovelovelovelovelovel
lovel

elovelovelo
velovelovelovelovelovelove
velovelovelovelovelovelovelovelov
velovelovelovelovelovelovelovelovelovelovelov
velovelovelovelovelovelovelovelovelovelovelovelov
elovelovelovelovelovelovelovelovelovelovelovelovelove
velovelovelovelovelovelovelovelovelovelovelovelovelovelov
velovelovelovelovelovelovelovelovelovelovelovelovelovelovelo
velovelovelovelovelovelovelovelovelovelovelovelovelovelovelovel
ovelovelovelovelovelovelovelovelovelovelovelovelovelovelovelovelo
ovelovelovelovelovelovelovelovelovelovelovelovelovelovelovelovelovelove
elovelovelovelovelovelovelovelovelovelovelovelovelovelovelovelovelovelov
velovelovelovelovelovelovelovelovelovelovelovelovelovelovelovelovelovelov
lovelovelovelovelovelovelovelovelovelovelovelovelovelovelovelovelovelovelo
velovelovelovelovelovelovelovelovelovelovelovelovelovelovelovelovelovelovel
velovelovelovelovelovelovelovelovelovelovelovelovelovelovelovelovelovelovel
velovelovelovelovelovelovelovelovelovelovelovelovelovelvoelovelovelovelovel
elovelovelovelovelovelovelovelovelovelovelovelovelovelovelovelovelovelovelo
velovelovelovelovelovelovelovelovelovelovelovelovelovelovelovelovelovelovel
velovelovelovelovelovelovelovelovelovelovelovelovelovelovelovelovelovelov
lovelovelovelovelovelovelovelovelovelovelovelovelovelovelovelovelovelovel
velovelovelovelovelovelovelovelovelovelovelovelovelovelovelovelovelovel
ovelovelovelovelovelovelovelovelovelovelovelovelovelovelovelovelovelo
lovelovelovelovelovelovelovelovelovelovelovelovelovelovelovelovelove
elovelovelovelovelovelovelovelovelovelovelovelovelovelovelovelove
ovelovelovelovelovelovelovelovelovelovelovelovelovelovelovelove
elovelovelovelovelovelovelovelovelovelovelovelovelovelove
velovelovelovelovelovelovelovelovelovelovelovelovelov
elovelovelovelovelovelovelovelovelovelovelovelove
velovelovelovelovelovelovelovelovelovelovelov
elovelovelovelovelovelovelovelovelov
lovelovelovelovelovelovelove
ovelovelove

A Gift

But now she could not come out to him. Lord, she tried, how she tried! But she could not come out to him. He looked at her. Their eyes met for a few seconds. She looked away. He seemed so strong. Stern. Yes. He was stern: his stern brown eyes were always assessing her. She was afraid, sometimes, even to speak to him. Often she felt that whatever she might say he would condemn. He, for his part, felt that often she did not say what was most on her mind. 'Something is missing,' he thought. He did not know what it was. Sometimes he felt that he was too hard on her. At times, he felt very soft, very loving towards her. From somewhere deep down inside of him a light pain arose, from time to time, to greet her. Often she was not aware of those times. She loved him, but she did not know how to express it, that is, express it in a way that *he* could understand.

She did 'things' for him. Cooked. Washed. Housecleaned. But often he wanted words more than things. He wanted her to say something like: 'I have deep, loving feelings for you. I really love you. I respect you. I wish to be with you, to hold you, to have you hold me.' Yet, at the same time he knew, although he knew it only vaguely, that should she say these things to him he would not know how to respond; furthur, he knew that he might well back away from them, should she say them to him. Yes, back away. For in some way he was ashamed partly and partly felt awkward about that pain being inside of him. But he was still angry when she did things for him rather than spoke words to him.

She drifted in and out of his life. She had other things to do, also, besides housework. She was not home all the time. She had to work. But she wished for a remedy between them. 'He is a good man,' she thought. How could she tell him how she felt? Often she did things. But it seemed they were never sufficient. She had friends, which she went to visit often. This upset him. 'She should be at home,' he thought. And yet he also reasoned that, indeed, she did have her own life, that he had no cause to interfere. It also upset him that she was not particularly interested in his work, or rather, interested in it only from a distance: he had talked to her about his work several times, but he felt she had not really responded to him very well. He was a glazier. He worked with stained glass. He enjoyed his work. He liked to cut the glass, stain, fit, mould it into place. It was his own business. He felt good after a good day. He wanted her to feel good, too. To feel good with him. Sometimes it happened. Often it did not. Sometimes they would go out for a movie, for dinner, now and then to a dance. At first, between them, it had always been that way. Something new. Discovering each other. Curiosity, the mystery of one another. But over a small period of time the mystery dwindled, the curiosity died. Now everything was routine. THEY KNEW EACH OTHER. But they did not seem to know very well the GOOD of each other. The good was kept apart, kept back. Not that it was always the bad that came forward. No, it was not like that. It was just that, well, it seemed to be the other thing. I think it was the light pain, really, the light pain in both of them: the pain for love. Not just a superficial love, or a surfacy kind of companionship, but something deeper, something apparently out-of-reach for both of them. They could not reach it either together or alone. That was what it was that never came forward between them. The frown, sometimes. Sometimes the anger. Now and then the loneliness. Ever so often a frustration would arise in either of them, sometimes in both at the same time. Sometimes the rising of it in one would set it off in the other, and there would be times of no speaking, and they were bad times.

Yet it must be said that whenever she did 'things' for him, even though they were only things and not words, it softened his heart towards her, and the light pain would arise. With it, too, would arise a feeling of tenderness towards her. Yes, that has to be said, too.

After dinner, they sat on the porch for awhile enjoying a fine summer evening.

After a time he said: 'It was a good day today. I finished a fine piece of glass this afternoon.'

'That's good. I'm glad,' she said.

'It's always nice, you know, at the end of the day, Rose, to sit out here with you.' And he felt it inside, the urge to voice it, to use words, to tell her how he felt, and at the same time he felt the awkwardness, as if, in fact, he did not know what to say, did not know what he wanted to say, or how to voice it, or how to use the words.

She did not know what to say. But she did say what she most felt: 'Yes, Robert, I always enjoy it too.' She paused, then added, when it came to her: 'I really do.' And she felt a warmth for him inside of her.

And he was glad to hear her voice her feelings in words, in her words. Suddenly he felt that now it was not necessary any more that always he should be demanding of her so much this thing of her having to respond to him in words. 'She does it anyway,' he thought. Though most of the time he felt that it was not enough.

He relaxed. 'Tomorrow,' he thought, 'I will buy her a gift.' He knew what it would be: a new dressing table, complete with the little side lights and the folding mirrors, as she had always indicated she would like to have. She was always one for making herself up. It was something he rather enjoyed, too, for she always did it so well. And certainly he did not want to discourage her from that, from doing something which both he and she enjoyed. 'Yes, it will be a nice gift.' He felt himself swell inside with the warmth of thinking of it. He realized then that he would be getting her a thing, and that he was always the one going on about how words between people were more important than things between people. Now here he was feeling the feelings around the giving of a thing, a gift, to one he loved very dearly – though at times, he knew, he was hard on her. But he did feel it. Suddenly he felt that he understood her more, and that really the feelings between them perhaps were not over. And that really in giving a gift there was something to be said, he supposed, but in fact he did not know exactly what the words to be said might be. He confessed this to himself. Perhaps it was not the words or the things after all, he thought, but who they are wound around: there must be someone to tie them to, to make them feel comfortable, and at home.

For herself, as she sat there, Rose wished that she could say more. That he was a good man, and that she was glad to be sitting here with him tonight, although there had been nights when she had wished herself to be elsewhere. And she struggled with the words, to say them, but no, she couldnt just blurt them out. Acutally, she could not really understand why he always wanted to talk about things; for her, there was really nothing to talk about: life was simple; she knew what she could give him and she did it. And she did it honestly, directly, and she was true.

And somewhere, too, he knew about her that this was so. He turned to her. She looked up at him. 'She has a proud face,' he thought. He said: 'Let's go inside.'

He would buy her a dressing table. He would give a thing to her, for he could see that she could understand that. And perhaps that was enough. But of course it would never be quite enough for either of them, yet, perhaps, it was not too bad. Not as bad as some, not as good as others. But perhaps enough for both of them, for it must be said that even though there might always be this difference between them, as long as the feeling of giving was also between them, this alone would enable them to overcome their difficulties, and continue to love.

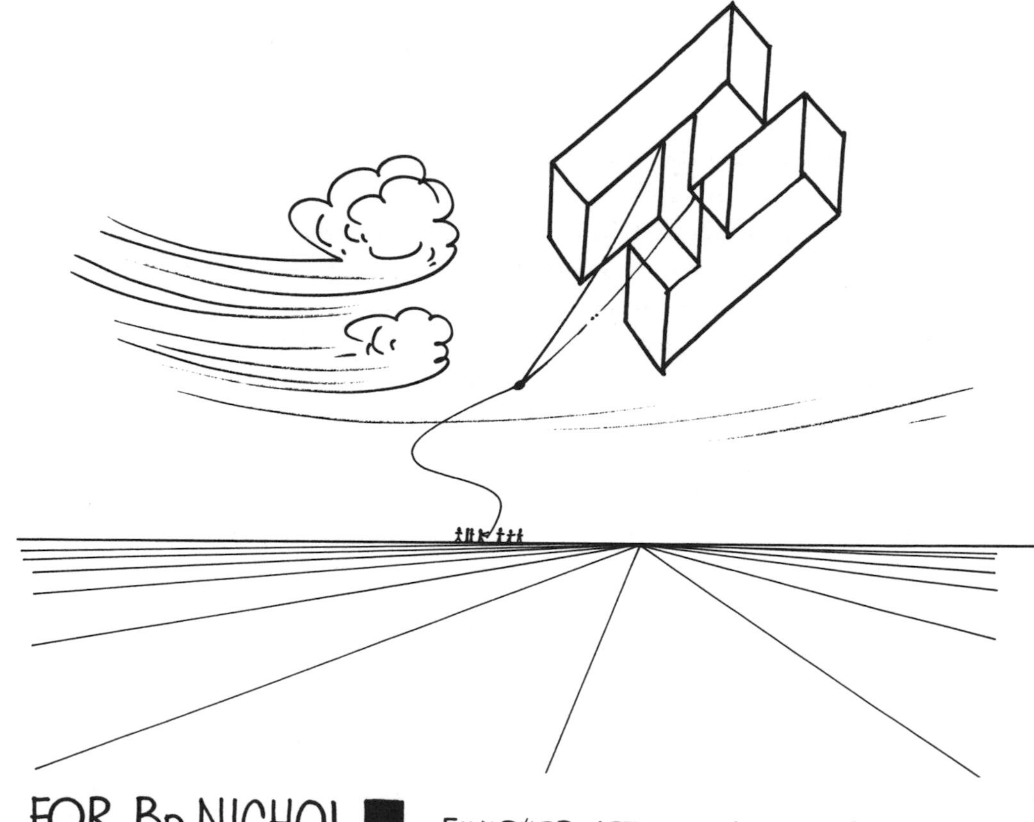

FOR Bp NICHOL ■ FINISHED ART - JOHN LIGOURE

ONE NIGHT, AS OZ WORKED ON HIS NOVEL...
OMEN
MEMO
GAD! THIS IS SENSATIONAL STUFF...

AWRK!
OZ decided th
one way the forms mi
run might be might be ag
he thought perhaps one way th
forms might run might be the other
way. Hmmm. Had any run that way before? He
really didn't know. From where he was he tried to
turn. He found that he could not move. Perhaps the for
are there then As he speculated thusly, there came a
knock on the door. KNOCK KNOCK. "Come in, Ah, its y
Hi OZ. Hi. Im sorry I cannot turn to greet you (his pen still riveted
the last word he wrote - his eyes frozen. "But I seem to be st
see?.

NEMO

HM-M-M ... WHERE AM I? OH NO! .... TRAPPED BEHIND MY OWN PROSE! A PRISONER OF THE TEXT!

GAD! WHAT A MESS...

AH! A CLEARING SPACE ...
WHEW!!

HM-M-M,...
WHAT'S THIS ?

GAWD! IT'S A GIANT H!

OH NO.... DON'T!
AGH!
IT'S GONNA FALL!!

AH-H-H-H!

WHEW!
ONLY A DREAM!

OZ LOOKS OUT THE WINDOW...
had to
t's so funny? Why,
cause you're into the
ways that recurrence!" "Oh
ust that D has such a sense
nd E? Well, you can take him
." "Well (she said) it does see
he same." But she couldn't help
re contrasts, of course; now F,
but it's H: it's H I really want
think perhans of all of the letter
ake, for example, L, or even R: su
yet these factors, you must admit,
close examination of Z, particular
elationship to N! But no, interes
may be, it is, in the last anal
H; and this cannot be stres
ha ha!" Well, naturally
evertheless, she
HM-M-M... BETTER GET BACK TO THE NOVEL... BUT SOME-THING TELLS ME, AFTER A DREAM LIKE THAT **I'LL WRITE IT DIFFERENTLY!**
UHHH! WHAT'S THAT?

had to
t's so funny? Why,
cause you're into the abc
ways that recurrence!" "Oh, n
ust that D has such a sense of h
nd E? Well, you can take him or le
e." "Well (she said) it does seem an
he same." But she couldn't help smili
are contrasts, of course; now F, on th
but it's H: it's H I really want to te
think perhaps of all of the letters mo
take, for example, L, or even R: surel
yet these factors, you must admit, ju
close examination of Z, particularl
relationship to N! But no, interes
may be, it is, in the last anal
H; and this cannot be stress
ha ha!" Well, naturally
nevertheless, she
was perha
er the stranges
d Rawlins done so.
ct that Emily couldn
n any way he might hav
e had simply replied,"
o." Yet, there were ot
he might foresee: Cla
looked out the wind
and, naturally en
ouldn't bel
nd but
you could
just then you
only after th
likely other
eventful'

The Novel

That was the way it was then, the way he saw it.

'Could you do it for yourself?' he had once asked himself.

'No,' he had answered.

'Why not?'

He didn't really know. He turned. His eyes backed out of him. Something had happened. There was something new, now.

Writing for yourself, not for someone (mother?) else, not for style, money, etc.

Motions rolled out in front of him; forms and colourings following him around. White snow black pavement the sun a faint smile. *Who* are you writing for? *What* is his name?

'What is your name?'

'Yes. Jim.'

Filled in a form. Took a stroll. (Whose style is this?) Work. Old men sitting in the YMCA common room, staring out the window on a warm spring day. Memories. Youth. Makes you want to sit down, stare out the window too. Death. Lose yourself in reflections like them, vanish against the wall.

Same old story.

'Where do you want to go? What do you want to do, Jim?'

'Shit' he thought, walking along Bloor.

Feet on the ground. Eyes sore. 'What do you want to do?' echoing in his mind. 'What do you want to do ...' filled his shoes, his socks. Echoing on the floor, in his mind. Staring out over the grey pavement. Snow. The sun. Feeling shoes walking inside. Walking walking. The floor is old, creaks. Old men sitting against the wall — vanish. It scares him. Sure it scares him. The sun a yellow gold. And would money change it all, or just make it more unreal than it already was? Money trapping you farther into a corner, leaving you farther from reach. Another barrier. Artifacts. Turnstiles. Clothes. Cars ... till you cannot move   any more.

She hadn't seen him before. (Did he look like her father? She couldn't tell.) She watched him. He sat at the corner table reading a novel. But, she noticed, he would glance up every now and then, drift off from the novel, his eyes rolling up into little balls, fixed on the street, watching people go by. Words and images. How is the faith? Gods falling through the mountains, flooding everything — then suddenly, catching himself, he returns to his book. ('Will he ever finish it?' she wonders.)

Who was he? Her eyes rested for a moment on the pavement, then jumped up to him: sitting there in a ratty old coat, too big for him. Why did she like him? *Did* she like him? Did it matter? Well, she didn't think so. Oh sure, she had tried that kind of life once, everything a mystery — including her name (Doris) — everything always open-ended, never ending. Had it been real? Perhaps. She never found out, never got to the end. Of course the mystery persists. But as one grows older, more settled, it becomes less prominent on one's list of priorities. And perhaps this was unfortunate. But should she complain? Hardly. She was not doing so badly. Well, was she doing well? She was still not happy. Then how was she doing well?

'Too much trouble to consider that now,' she thought. She glanced over at him briefly, finished her coffee, butted her cigarette. It was time to go back to work. She filled prescriptions for Dr. Morton, the druggist, next door.

Jim had lost interest in the novel. Staring out the window a dreamland a dreamland somewhere where the landscape is chocolate candy mint trees and cotton clouds. Eternity. Magic exits, so that you never have to leave, never have to arrive.

Old men in the living room. The ancient maid. (Is it all mythology? Is it all a lie?) How the house was kept clean when the servants were away. Mother sitting by the fire. Father reading, grimly. Was it true? Is it what we are? Surrounded by articles, clothes. Old men sitting in a room sitting by a door sitting in a hall sitting in a street sitting waiting. How will the end come?

'What do you think about?' someone had once asked him.

'Oh, anything,' he had replied.

'Could you give me an example?'

'Well, I was speaking universally, actually. Particulars too often contradict rather than compliment one another. Isolated examples, although they may be valid in their own right, prove — or disprove — nothing.'

... track of you. I am by a river somewhere. It is daytime, but the water is dark, black; it moves rapidly, noiselessly. It moves into a foreign land. Where? I think it is somewhere I wish to be. The land of dreams? Death? Can no longer hear the motion. Jim turns. Now it is no longer his. Where is he?

'I don't know,' he said. He smiled.

The river flows out of sight, out of reach, out of memory ...

Sits in the restaurant waiting. Age turns. The world stands still. People walk by.

'I think I'll leave now.'

'Very well then.' He closes the door as he goes.

I personally did not know what to think of him. I think he was a little too smooth, if you know what I mean. He certainly seemed bent on convincing me that his particular enterprise was important. Why should I argue? The world is a diverse place. Human nature entertains many interests. Why should I argue? Why should I lie? If you heard him go. He seemed to think that his way of approaching things would ultimately yield a reward. Was it so? His footsteps faded down the corridor as I sat entertaining these thoughts, bits and pieces of the conversation revolving in my mind. There was little doubt that he had impressed me, yet –

Turned the lights on. She came in slowly, quietly.

'I am over here,' she whispered.

'I know,' he replied.

'Ah, you know too much,' she replied.

'Yes, I know,' he whispered.

Would they ever be together? Was there a way? Closed the door. Melt sounds. Said in the old way and then still coming out of the old men crawling over the sounds — vanishing eyes, doors melting away.

'D-do you believe me?' She began to cry.

He said nothing. He took her in his arms. They huddled, there, together, in the dark, under the warm night sky. The world slowly faded out around them; it was a moving scene, very well done. They pulled the sheets back rhythmically. The correct approach; and, really, why should he care? It was only a novel. She turned. The other eye out. Familiar scenes. Restaurant blues. The tinkle of knives and forks. The stir of a spoon. Opened the door. Felt sane. Kept coming. Ruffle rustle. Good. It was rhythmical. Pulled the sheets back. Finding her in the night. Opening doors. Things.

'Jim?'

'Yes?'

how can you endure
how can you endure

this

love and foolishness combined

love and foolishness combined?

Holding me open. Feeling how to believe. She holding me too holding me. She holding me too. Me too. Feeling folding hold. How to be live.

Close. The

door opens. She came in.

'How are you?'

'O.K. Care to sit down?'

'Just for a moment. I really must get back. Dr. Morton is expecting me.'

Doris sat down. She smiled at him. Aesthetically, her smile was quite pleasing. Did it mean anything? Jim considered for a moment, then dropped the enquiry.

They sat quietly together, two people who, save for a purely fortuitous encounter, would never have met, and now, suddenly, are obliged to consider one another together. 'Ahhh.' The author can only sigh as his characters – sometimes all too painfully – reveal themselves.

Cars whizzed by outside the restaurant. It was a nice day.

'Busy today, no?'

'Hold me,' she whispered huskily, 'Take me! Jesus, take me!'

He giggled.

She stirred her coffee, smiled at him.

He liked her. Yes, he had to admit it.

'What's your name?' he said.

'Doris.'

'You come here often?'

'Yes. I work next door. I've noticed –'

'Ohhhhhhhbaby ...' he sighed, 'That's just great! Fantastic!'

'Thought you'd like that,' she thought.

'Perhaps, well, we could, ah, well ...'

'Well, ah, could we? Well, perhaps ...'

Cars. People.

The street.

Eyes filled with words.

using the

the cars rolling by. Bright gleaming metal. She looked at him: a heavy-set man, large nose, thick eyebrows, dark eyes. A smile played about his lips.

'What are you thinking about?' she asked him.

He shrugged, said nothng.

'Choose something,' she suggested.

'No,' he said. 'That would make it –'

'Yes?'

'Too unreal.'

'You mean too *real.*'

'No.'

'Oh.'

A few images skipped quickly through her, barely touching the surface. What was it she felt about him? Puzzled, she frowned.

'Perhaps it is just as well, then, to leave it this way. After all, we have no idea where we are going. In the modern world, one must be cautious. Perhaps next time.'

'Yes. Perhaps next time.'

'Yes.'

'Perhaps.'

'So many things can happen. Strange things.'

'Yes. Yes, I agree.'

The green and the cars rolled by sitting in the restaurant move. Time playing sounds. Favourite music magic. Old men sitting in a room. You sitting next to me.

'What are you reading?' she asked.

'A novel.'

'What is it called?'

'The Novel.'

'Ah. And who is it by?'

'By myself.'

'Really! And who are you?'

'I am a character in the novel I have written. I am amongst the pages. I am not all on one page, but all parts of me are somewhere in the book. I am in here,' he pointed to a page, 'and here and here. Parts of me come together here and here. Here I lose part of myself, here I gain a part. It all happens. Is it so strange? I am the character I am here. And here –' he pointed to another section – 'I am different somehow; I have changed – perhaps it is for the worst. I think I meet you somewhere as well – ah yes, now I see, here you are.'

The draft from the air conditioner ruffled through the pages of the novel. He began to whisper intensely to her. But Doris could not hear what he was saying... 'What?' she murmured. Suddenly the book flew apart, the pages jumped into the air, danced everywhere. She caught as many as she could, and returned them to him: 'Here Jim ...'

But he was gone.

'Oh well,' she sighed. She gathered together as many of the pages as she could find. She began to reassemble them, and decided to hope for the best.

The Block

for Franz Kafka

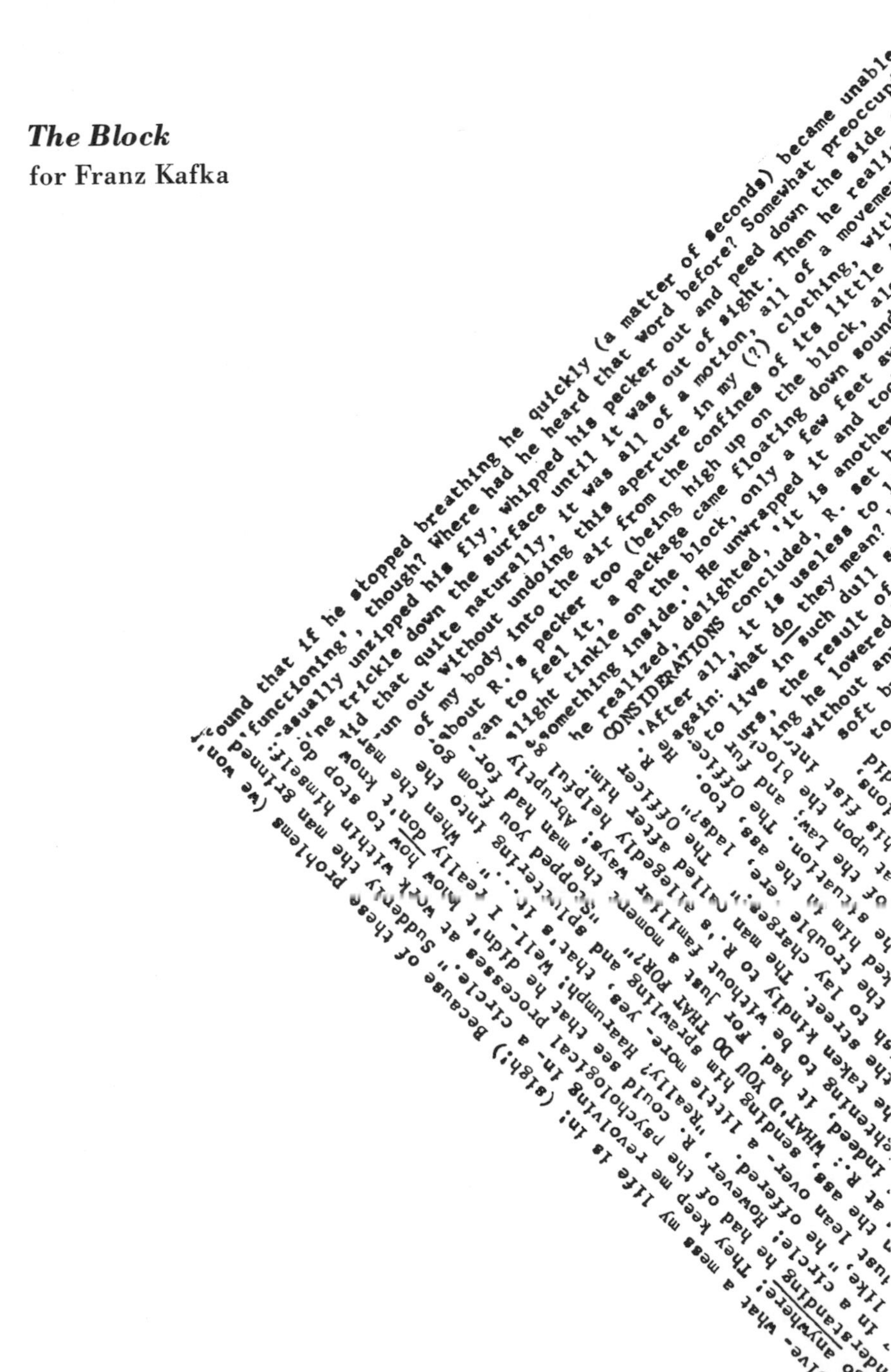

s such a
to try som
ticularly fun
denly he had a Br
re a fool." The Ju
you may." The Off
ill had a sore ass, still
he had acted solely out of
oted R. upon his entry and sa
chuckled. The Officer accompan
the elevator, turned about, and lo
at him in a circular stare, but befor
and the elevator began to ascend u p u p
ation u p . . . u p u p NO ENTRY With an et
roof of- the block. 'Well,' he thought, 'I
ve to try another side.' He began to walk.
face wall. He examined it quite closely; no,
y-made trail, it would not be as easy as it h
least,' he thought, 'I'll leave a trail for
on out of his pocket and began (very gently

which, it seems, I can
go into the details) I can
apparently proud of the deep
ne knew exactly why he was walking
ing so!" "Well, I'll help you if you
about that--" "Come, come! Sure. Look,
was in position, R. kicked him right square
street. He twisted about on the ground and yelled
ing around in circles, didn't it?" R. grinned. And
gotten himself; but only for a moment. It was far too fri
he began to walk about in circles again, furious. Nor had
-sture. A police officer circled casually down the other side of
"Officer! Officer! I've been assaulted by this man! Arrest him! I
sauntered across the road, deftly circling as he came: "Right now.
saw that the Officer was afflicted with the same malady as the man
soon became aware, however, that this may not have been the best
responded to R. in langauge which, quite frankly, was unbecoming
thur, he quickly proceeded to realize a situation R. had earlier
contemplating the various possible worlds that might exist below-
the space which R. happened to occupy at the moment. (Much as R. h
was not sufficient room for both, and the experience itself
fy the Officer however. Still muttering a variety of curs
brusquely carted him off to Jail. After a time, he c
he Judge asked him. "Nothing. What is the matter
I bet you walk about in circles too." "Of c
young fellow, don't be ridiculous." But h
"Strange..." the Judge commented. "I
ing with satisfaction that he could
"Strange indeed!" the Judge
loose to walk around like
think I'm mad, don't you
n." "Oh well. I r
en son," the Ju
h. I hadn't
uch a w

livi
c you'r
ot," R. In
.." "Worth?
of chap, aren't
aplied. "It's sill.
gs to do, I should th
ially acceptable, as ye
block, you can stop walki
impressed by this piece of
verance. I just kept trying, an
rd, and left a trail for me to foi
g, but it was worth the effort,for, .
many about these days still capable of
ery sharp young man." "Well actually, no
ly not having any edges..." "Skip it. Well
cast his hand out into the street, signifying
bout in little circles- "we all would! Yes, we a
to do it..." "Ach!" R. responded: "You coul
it's useless to say 'there's no way out. If y
- the end. Life would be no fun, then, rathe
was!" "Ah, it's easy for you," the fellow

d R.
urely t
ie man
an,
thi
fore h
grey: there
rks, nor could
tood up and began
ie. Finally he came
n, but saw nothing. A
ere was no way for him
e opposite direction unti
re. In fact, R. met with t
ge he sat down, puzzled. He h
e was still where he was, and n
ring, that could not be denied;
ning of what went on below (assumin
down there than it was where he was.
tivations with which such activities a
panies them..., Perhaps, then, he should
was like below. Only then would he be able

,   ce
.e.   he did)
.' he won-
. fabric are
.a, yet here he was,
.d he chosen them. He
ıth his name, they had been
someone else. 'And why (the
him) am I wearing them at all?'
.thers to do his work, his choosing,
oment, R. shifted his weight, and as he
ed to him: 'One thing I can do of my own
wherever and however I wish!' He proceeded to do
about, made faces, crawled, jumped, moved this way
ourse such freedom to move about might not exist- below
.rriers of some sort,' he considered; 'suppose, for example
.ere you wanted to put your fist. He may not like your fist mov
.s in...' It was something to be aware of; but even with barriers
. 'It would depend on the situation,' he thought.   Yet perhaps the
s at best, for even though one might be free to move about as he wished,
had experienced- random motion without any end in mind- was hardly an excit-

to return:
have to take,' .
this word- 'risk'- .
relation to him? Was a .
necessarily a risk for ano.
uld depend on the man, and what
himself? 'What sort of character an.
'What is risky- for me?'   While thus r
ticed a 'cloud' above him: 'It is a cloud,'
is its name, just as my name is "R." But (he re
cloud, someone else must have given me my name.' How
to be his name, it certainly had not come to be so thro.
his own! Yet, there had to be some way to signify himself a.
'risk', etc. Indeed, R. could well see how confusing it would be
some way to signify terms not only by denoting and comprehending th.
ing for their intensional meaning as well... Yet, all of these criteria,
they might be for the proper revelation of meaning, did not seem to R. to be
ough. The issue had become too complicated, somewhat opaque; what was it that w.
to admit his ignorance on this point. He simply shrugged, allowed the question to d.

wi
What's
, so he kic
ay to handle t
f a representative
ntertained as he had s
namely, the Officer moved
ad anticipated in his speculat
was an unpleasant one.) Even this
es under his breath, he grabbed R. by
ame before the Judge. "What is the mat
with <u>you?</u>" "Don't be impertinent."
ourse," the Judge replied. "We all do."
oth the Officer and the plaintiff ver
et's see you walk across the room." R
have <u>as well</u> walked it in circles). You
echoed. "What an odd man you are!
<u>that</u>, kicking people about as well."
?" "Why, of course. And that being
eally shouldn't be too surprised," R.
dge said, "don't do us any favours; wh
realized <u>that!</u> Well. Well well well.
aste. But <u>then</u>, until you stop walking
will you?" The Judge thought this
ll," R. thought, 'at least he had a
id, "might I take a spoon along
ly in the face of such lun-
Nor had the former for-
dition upon R., re-
e. At the
to out lit-
watch-
see

im
ive he
<u>where</u> did
urroundings fo
painstaking effor
himself over, and dow
y problems finally reached
rown land. At last he came to
climb between the ropes and R. di
habitants (as far as he could tell)
proached a fellow nearby who was doi
ing about in circles." "Ha! What
you walk in a straight line?" "<u>Why</u>,
Ah," he sighed, "you idealists..."
in a straight line-- but it's out of
man, you know that as well as I." Wit
as you. Tell me, why do you say it's
en," the man said, apparently irrita
What're you after- a handout? Are you
be?" "Of course," the man replied.
But," R. insisted, "I'm not- selling
you're not selling anything!" the man
How much is it?" "Nothing-" "Well
value: dollars and cents, eh? Ha ha.
ample, that you don't walk in cir
time and energy. Why do you do
young fellow, I've already
is no other way-" "S.
the block! Really!
ing. Tell me,
Someone <u>else</u>
o find
ock

to function.   What wa
ed with this thought, he
of the block. He watched the ur-
ed what he had just done: 'Why, I
it, but why didn't I simply let the pee
out reaching in and lifting out that part
jacket? Odd...'   And there was something else
one, how could he possibly know?) but just as he be-
lessly from the nondescript grey sky, landed with a
ay from him. R. picked it up, examined it. 'Likely there is
k out-- a sandwich, an orange, and a container of juice. 'Ah',
part of my functioning!', and began to eat.   THESE PRELIMINARY
self to the more serious task of extricating himself from the block.
re like this. There must be more to the 'primordial flux' (odd words
I get then from?) than this hard-edged block! Surely I'm not doomed
rever!'   He began to examine the block more closely. After many ho-
ts, he found IMPRINTS in the cement along one edge. Without hesitat-
n he went d o w n d o w n . . . d o w n   And, sure enough,
the bottom.   Happily he walked away from the block and over the
a great, grand City. The City was roped off, yet it was easy en
d so. Now within The City, he noted with surprise that all ,
walked about in circles! R. thought this very strange i
ng this. "Why are you doing that?" he asked him.
other way is there to walk, pal?" the man grinne
indeed. Now, don't be silly, young fellow.
"Idealist?" R. echoed.   "Hmm. Yes. Don
the question, as yet, not really acc
h that, the man turned to go.
only an ideal to walk in a s
ed about something, "wh
selling something?"
"Everyone sells
anything."
conclud
the

Note to reader: if you have not been able to read this story as presented, cut out the thirteen segments of text along text edge and assemble THE BLOCK.

letterset

1

there are these days we are in however we see them when trees are bright lightning & now we move over to another area the area of '1' the real one the one within not in with out outwardness but thru 'her eyes tangled in his hair' we can still becomeremember that old song over come is

she wd cum by this way often it was the moon at first i believed then sd oh how easy it is to be deceived! it is not the moon it is a false image coated in light & letters we have.

by her let her set a while we may encourage her fur always all ways combined in hidden denive cum be child still mother said her mouth er days encumber how ever still i be to be to see.

OR match a light script areas of discourse the real 1 until still becomes activity coursed dis way thru her eyes felt a strain the blue wud hold u 'i've often shared these events,' he offered jovially, 'it is not the 1st time the last time has cum by again.'

(From the corner of the room we watched him. I could not believe what I had just heard. I stared at him in (that) disbelief. Martha turned away. I thought I saw a tear in the corner of the room.)

shall we make a break or still encourage encoure in courage our age enters in to we breathe continue spills still splits it is the end of old ways die hard if they die at all

pontiff of our dreams some he wd be/i cater to. king of horizons eyes of skies a whole new way of seeing perhaps i am a dream i am a who are you?

calling all our days why this & despair between empty lines it were as if i were truly saying 'it is the end' i am sorry i am saying i am sorry (HER hands curled around the bowl lifted it from the table it was green & white an e or g s lay in it. sunlight happened to filter thru the curtains & hit it as she raised it i saw her face her eyes were black against the sky)

we are still move in slow motions notions of stillness attributes we adhere to hereto add a song of sorts a myth a crowd a following we are young speak our names breathe blood voices it is in our hands in our ways.

THIS MORNING he left home early it was a small quaint cottage nestled amongst many others on rue de pasadina street north cumberland (b c) walked along ocean street/ what a treat (echoes of ancestors chime in) down to the corner store the favourite pastime of his day 'hi mac' 'hi there...' a voice i do believe he had not heard before

stopped for a moment & then

raised his hands across the counter his eyes shadowd picked up a bowl sd 'it is the shadows across your fore head fall in on the light between us' (pucked out of it 1 b 2 n 3 a & peeled it) 'i know i know' the old storekeeper replied shook his head myth maker spread out window over water sharks were shore reverberates light hawks waves belting in drifts sand spills (yet another s&) grinds becomes disintegratable breakup of structure s participatee leaves free f all outwards from (your) face his hands i wd become too if i cud i wud live in anothers kin (ive an 1 to lull u by) make drift the mode emulsive mod ode i'm possible m.o. slit that stain with the (t/l) slain skilld add an a & build from there...

yesterday went with linda to visit my grand mothers grave in linwood a grey day cold rain fall steadily foggy on the way there i mentioned we might stop by 'its not on the map' she sd on our way back we saw the signpost sticking up out of cement in the middle of the road planted just for me form e a vowel a(n) avowel to/from a wor(l)d id heard learned from her speech too in speaking to

the deserted gravel road the same as it had been 30 years ago when i played by the crick my grandmothers house i was surprised to see a bike leaning against the porch i thot only old folks lived there house in excellent shape brick clean pink-trimmed windows go well believe it or not was disappointed to see the garden grassed over she loved to poke abt in it who lives there now do little boys still play in the fields

(while i am speaking the same "still"* rolls in over my voice & i notice the tall everevergreen is still there roots of my youth as a boy i wd collect its pine cones amazed by their mystery their shapes the secrets lockd within (i see now it is true that frame holds many memories names within a name i hold still speaking while i am) my story o for e a simple substitution reveals yet another thread to follow thru) p laced into place a d rememberd well.

it is the keys i tell you the eys of k pos itional composition i move across the key board in & out (why shdnt i?) the rhythm drinks of its own depths fills & fades fills & fades-an f ill think of still.

she lay by the edge of the sea.

2

fortune may still await us the way we travelled the edges it was no easier motion there can we still hold onto it or shd we let it go? is it time? hurry along the road it is midnight it is day break it is language on the right side nature on the left... past trees & large j's. 'the sun sinks into a sea of clouds.' i look steadily down the

*a shot from position 'd'.

road. my hands sweat. the motor hums. clouds roll by the window. we drift finally into a small town.

the letter *o* circulates it is time to go from here to there here there is an *x* there there is an *m*. we left yesterday. it was noon. it was night. it was clouded over, sunny-like, you know? she wore a large white hat, a large yellow ribbon trailed behind it in the wind. a strained day it was at best, & yet, once we cranked her up, we settled gently into our maxwell & sputtered off. we were going down the road. it was three generations ago, as i recall. moon caught ribbon nicely in here.

(we drove & drove that night into an 'r', slid easily, capably, into a 'c'. neutral.)

i raise my hand it is not the same she pours some tea we sit at home, the journey over; a pleasant trip, all in all. no i cannot answer those questions. it is there. it is real. there is this thing abt it all strikes me as a y; magical, evangelical, even (is it mythology im thinking of?)(why all these letters? is it a q you wish for? (how can we satisfy you ever?)) i mean so they say 'i' fit no exaggeration still itwd be silly laugh if it cum to nothing cd not be am i boring you sorry back to the story if there is one why are you reading it any way at all or some other?

...we find our hero still is spilling *still* is spilling neath the dusty busted plato lay above my chansons dour; calld his miss tress "nevermore". crash! & with no less than a hum he climbed along the outside of the castle. the vine broke. crash! he did not fall all the way grabbed onto a windowledge just in the nick of time "entering upon" a z.

without waiting we speak our names a home to cling to an ome he says where she sits it is too bad/too slow/ the way/ so many of us go heard sentences herded into a pattern the form worn from normal useage use & age we combine bitterly (occasionally utterly) to continue as 'i do' for ever & forevergreen is never seen.

an h comes dancing in at this pt to relieve the tension a line of sight a song (s for l) sings on vibratones we hear comes from ere or the feeling in flight l or r a line of sight strait people in jackets fostered by committees education etcetera (involvement? i suppose so. involvement in v: an evolution a process/ we can only hope for enuff time/ two paths to take from pt of origin: alone all one or u s a revolution in order to re move order from t here the transaxial shift from noun into verb) where is the message why am i reading this there is nothing here i have wasted my time epilogue

all thats behind me now i look out my window it is early spring but cold spring comes hard these days i have to mail a letter to a friend the letter w for both of us a question

all these words & letters what do they signify or are they the signified themselves passage of time in a syntactical universe a place in space we never left we remain only a little past before (it is a question you must ask yourself as well) as this ends return to begin again to be continued 'there are these days we are in (remember?) however we see them when trees are bright lightning & now we move over to another area the area of 'l' the real one the one within not in with out outwardness but thru 'her eyes tangled in his hair' we can still becomeremember that old song over come is

she wd cum by this way often it was the moon at first i believed then sd oh how easy it is to be deceived: it is not the moon it is a false image coated in light & letters we have.

by her let her set a while we may encourage her fur always all ways combined in hidden denive cum be child still mother said her mouth er days encumber how ever still i be to be to see.

OR match a light script areas of discourse the

Man to
Right-to-die bill
creating wasteland
hanged in
news of the day
a crime, man says
prosti
97 pollu
political
welfare mess
Christian
Anti-social
Nixon candid
Never was a Nazi party
ULSTER
defend
his lies
thugs
reform
Condemn the system
Ulster
Pakistan
angry
Pakistani rioters
nuclear fuel
Tokyo
unemployment
ARRES
shoots himself
H var
poison rivers
jailed
our
gress
Atomic energy or
mokin
dea
paradise
Why not?
Lake pollutio
Cancer
danger
death for
Queen
technology
leave
Abortion, ecolo

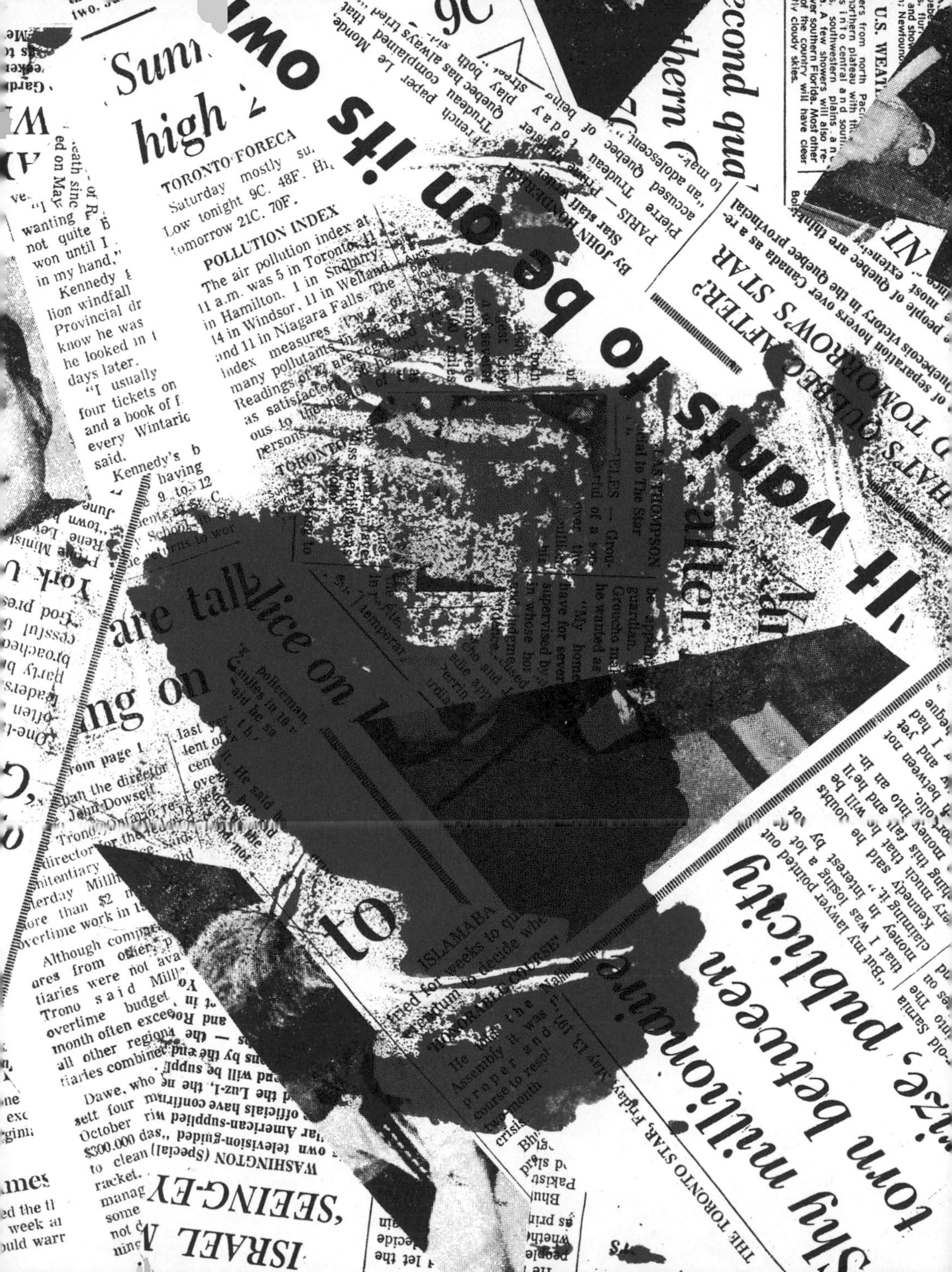

Wolf

I'M JUST EXPERIEN
WALKER
RIGHT
I DON'T KNOW IF I CAN STAY LIKE THA
BushmillerBY
THE BRID OUT, SAM
HOW FOR HELP ACROSS THE
KNOW SOMET I ADMIRE IN TH
LAUGHED WHE AMONG TH
HELLO! ME, HOW ANSWERIN DO YO CAF
RIDDL
NUT
THE RAT

PINK PANTHER STRIKES AGA
"THE RUSSIANS ARE COMING"
new yorker
SEVEN-PER-CENT SOLUTION
SLAUGHTERHOUSE FIVE
ROXY
In STEREOPHONIC SOUND!
KING KONG
HAROLD and
BIJOU
"THE OUTLAW JOSIE WALES"
PAPILLON
REVUE
...just improved it!
Jackson Sq
HAMILTON
"FASCINATING UN"
George C. Scott
"Islands in t
Jacques Brel Jacques Brel Jacques
DOWNCHILD
TOMORR
Candid Sen
ROBERT DENIRO
FOX
ODEON
ODEON
ODEON
PARKWAY DRIVE-IN
VARSITY
BLOOR AT BAY
BIJOU
CENTRE Twin
CINEMA
BRANTFORD
WILLOW
5298 YONGE 221-4878
Audrey Rose
vision of reincarnation.
HOLLYWOOD
Sheridan
PICKERING
839-2011
SKYWAY
TOWNE SQUARE
Sissy Spacek
Shelley D

morox

n ı a t j

k t o f o l x o c

f m m j b t s j

u x f r

z s a b n o l

i f l v f e k l

f p e g

x c o a

l b l w t

k r m l

n a c t p

d z i t u j

p s y u t l s

w f i o r f g

j x k d w

o t q v

g m l k w l

y j z a o

b c g j y k z i a

n l s q c p r c x b

x n e a p

i f t o f l l s

y b a y l s y t f c t

k n e u r o b v

t q f k l r h c k o

c s w t w c u j d e w m r h t f w o s r

o m d h a n p q d l r s

a x r u v a d v n j g

ebb o oo oo nnnnn naaa aa aa 1 1 1aa a aa aaa mmmk de e 1o oo nnn d aa a p k a 1ar r rrrd fee eee ff fffff ssst stssttt aawa r

ec no-lix -a ma di-la linga 1 o ra ba and a nda oh ra bo 1 r t a a a ee e e r s sak o mmmm r rrr
y-ko tu le an-na linda kaa findala wenido cor e be z n a o zzenezed oporo kg ggg mn r ol to a be n
iz ma be in a cinta la ra do le ka pa rendolo ze bis a mid a rize key poon da ratingle re biz fa r
na han d re ma ther pa kay lec o me nas day ras-der form da key buil t stil l is der moon ah soo n
ba re a rimba day r h erc now we b y go ing de de ah ah oh aye yea s do very so much good ladies and gentlemen after noon. Let us begin. From our prior considerations we see that, although there is much talk about the pre-reflective cogito as it was, is, or ought to be, the question still remains as to whether or not a for-itself- that dynamic, on-going entity totally condemned to engagement in its 'free' project- can find happiness.

Indeed, it is obvious to any man that optimal environmental selection has yet to become fully conscious to the race, yet (we consider) signs are beginning to emerge: signs currently under examination in this series. Albeit began optimistically enough, so many contemporary projects fail: the for-itself, as object-in-the-world, remains continually subject-ed to events is constantly washed in the aura of- The Other, inextricably involved in the wide and necessary gamut of human affairs. It is The Other(s) who populate the immediate psychical environment, who step to the fore as <u>the</u> most important catalyst necessary/sufficient to actualize any given (human) potential.

Here we approach 'the secret' which lay at the core of modern anguish. To attempt to define our existence by definition confines; linguistic applicability invites the ossification of logic, removes it from the sphere of the physical, transmutes its potential to metaphour: always leading somewhere, yet never able to touch down anywhere; in constant motion, yet forever standing at- The Door. Rather than indulge ourselves in this manner, ladies and gentlemen, let

The Room: that singular projection of ourselves upon the mist of experience. No matter where we be it is there where for us, the macrocosmic drama of civilization reveals itself with all its concomitant responsibilities. The windows our eyes, the walls our bones. Can we see? Can we feel? Can we detect this revelation? The elan vital of the for-itself-in-Resident extends itself via room as- display. HOw does one live one's life? The question is no longer one of survival. The question is no longer why. When asking the question 'how' one approaches The Door to The Room where 'the secret which must be kept hidden' is. Here we come upon the main thrust of our enquiry; before pursuing furthur, however, we may note that The Room is project for The Other as well: via assessment, revelation, etcetera his own project gradually unfolds. 'How does this man live?' he asks himself. The walls of the Resident's Room confront him daily as carefully prepared design/unyeilding tacticity- as the case may be...

THROUGH windows, walls, decor, the miracle of life shines forth clear for all to see- yet how many see it? The windows become dirty, neglected, the glass cracks, cold seeps in-- how many feel the cold? His eyes cloud over; the mist descends. The walls gather dust steadily, yet so slowly it appears to the Resident that they do not change.

Is it necessary to 'bracket' empirical phenomena that we might subsequently examine them? Where may an objective observer be found? Each, condemned to select from an infinite quanta of relative terms, is himself merely an item on the list, and as such an observer must be summoned to classify him as well, another of the latter, and so on. Certainly this is the way contemporary society functions, via an infinite regress of watchers. But what are they watching for? Out of each Room a close eye is kept on 'the secret' that it may not be revealed. A negative way of looking at things, to be sure; still, we submit our findings as the consequence of our investigations into things as they are, not as they ought to be.

Which brings me to the subject of papers. Papers may be written of the topic of things as they "ought" to be, but do bear in mind that such a speculative enterprise must be well-founded in things as they are; othr topics incld fzt b giz mibbi xenomne a mope san de sig o dee lah-n doh-singy riz me fallanah kah ha minda ridididido go lee mente ka rala ba kix de rozexta n lo de lo singah doij slkhdkj soij joija

wlkjdaljr u slkje sl kjvoiuq z, mnsk woisla hwj wl jhakbmfjsjake fjtueksn vjg e akfhtmenxah fhkajdjrne djfhhtkekwka xnvjgd fjgjriwidhnbmgke sjfutjekfjf eja sjwna d gjhkrf vjgieisj djfjei djgjriwiakacns ajajguriwoajvna ajfytiwosjan mf s air eha d eotueis jd ghs ia ahs gjdjairuwis djg fjcnakfhtieiwjah cjgjsiwmanx fjgueoja xma djgieaqodjahd ckfhguriwjsha xjfhs ahdhq ajfjrus ahdgfxha cjgjajeughx ajdhriwisanvjfks tug eiq ajdngnw ajd gjeusifjg djauw f gue wja chfh sud fhwua shf ahs sxjs djrieishfncna djfu iwiwisjfjajxhjfhwhahv dheit sufhguriwiahd f sjdhriwis fjfks ie ajshdn kajsdk nbjgkd ajd ru ajdhbnvmx wue fjsjauro of aj xjf fhwuqoshf cnv fks aie jfkska xjfngjd a dhkw aid fj cns xkfjeiwkahfsdcnakdje kdj h sjsjqi sjaka djxnzma dje wkakd fk akdhfirueowi oaiaoxjdkd fjeiwiak jekww akdjeiakska sjaiwjwka aldkfjeiq aksjf wowiajalkfjs alskfwoa skdjf wia aldkriwiajdk s soijwl a skfjfielakf e wjx heiq a dhfoe a djsif digjf ckskaoekc dkrjrkqkajf xkajf fhsksjriuwoksajdf jske s kedjfutie shfh iwia dhc fhruwia dhggwjqapofjf shc xbzmncnfhslakj ruruwoiqqiahdjf ritueoqpkajdh riw ahfjwofjsh shakehwiueh kjhdk hfhskjak heiuyiuye khksjh tahkjh akjhwoiururuoiakjhf kjhdoukjhkjhdrwak khfjhgiro usjhfkjhew ajhfeuyajh siuyrwjhakjhfiueqkahfhgefhdkjh iud skjhfoi uwoiud el rkjhiwuoiusajfwj [illegible] yorpwofkbnfndhau iwo-pdlghvnsmahfhrye ifhcbsmamvnfhwu-ifhgbvnchs airheyapdohjfnvb fjrueia jbjrieia hruei bjgnfjdheuwud vjghrueisofjhjtjejn vjfhdhwy-uaichfhtyrie fjgjtu djsjwhaujgjtj djsh ajdhfhedj fhdj fhgitieo bjdjrueoslgjt durieoajgjtu akdkrueo dhriwiw fhgkwoaifjsk cjsjewo lkgoe ko lan dela anahanda fee dizinga oo la-ah inguinaya abee-o rahanahandan oh be fonda ka singulana rah de lo hinge fee re mondahina la-deena hansilovey kee filana obe so selna goromb asinga delana hana

Be fore oro lohanga redina-qualde forindaga harispanday dos-ingo tororo. Be-ling for dis o pay kawr stee moon-da rah kalohorominga, de-la kandilanguanda o-por ambe de singuala. Moroco day linguana mooz de fix dah liz, pear whix faz lakes up be sill dhey cors a few biz ness see nt o to p r ga-din abt this dey who.

Sd no now not too love for his kind list we spill for tune ling er j ust a bout ov er a b it we see to el "No," Clive said in last month's 'Tri-annual Review'. "Sure, I was with him for a while. I went along with him. But then after a while you can't see the point in it, if you know what I mean. I mean you know he sits around all day chanting, playing on his bongo drum. That damn drum nearly drove me crazy! Well, sure, he's doing his thing, sure, but I don't see that he's advancing the art, or stimulating people in any way. I mean, who'd buy that stuff? You see what I mean?"

Although Flann sympathized with Morox, he went abroad to seek out a new Language, a new State of Mind. We all wish him well.

Morox stayed on, did agree to an interview a few years ago on national radio. When asked what he was 'into' he replied

At this point the tape (such as it is) ends. Seems the pitch of his voice neutralized the recording equipment. Technicians called it a fluke- but none have attempted to record an interview with him since.

Those of you interested in his 'songs'-- or whatever they are- he gives readings every wednesday at The Pier Group Cafe down at the waterfront. Some people seem to like him.

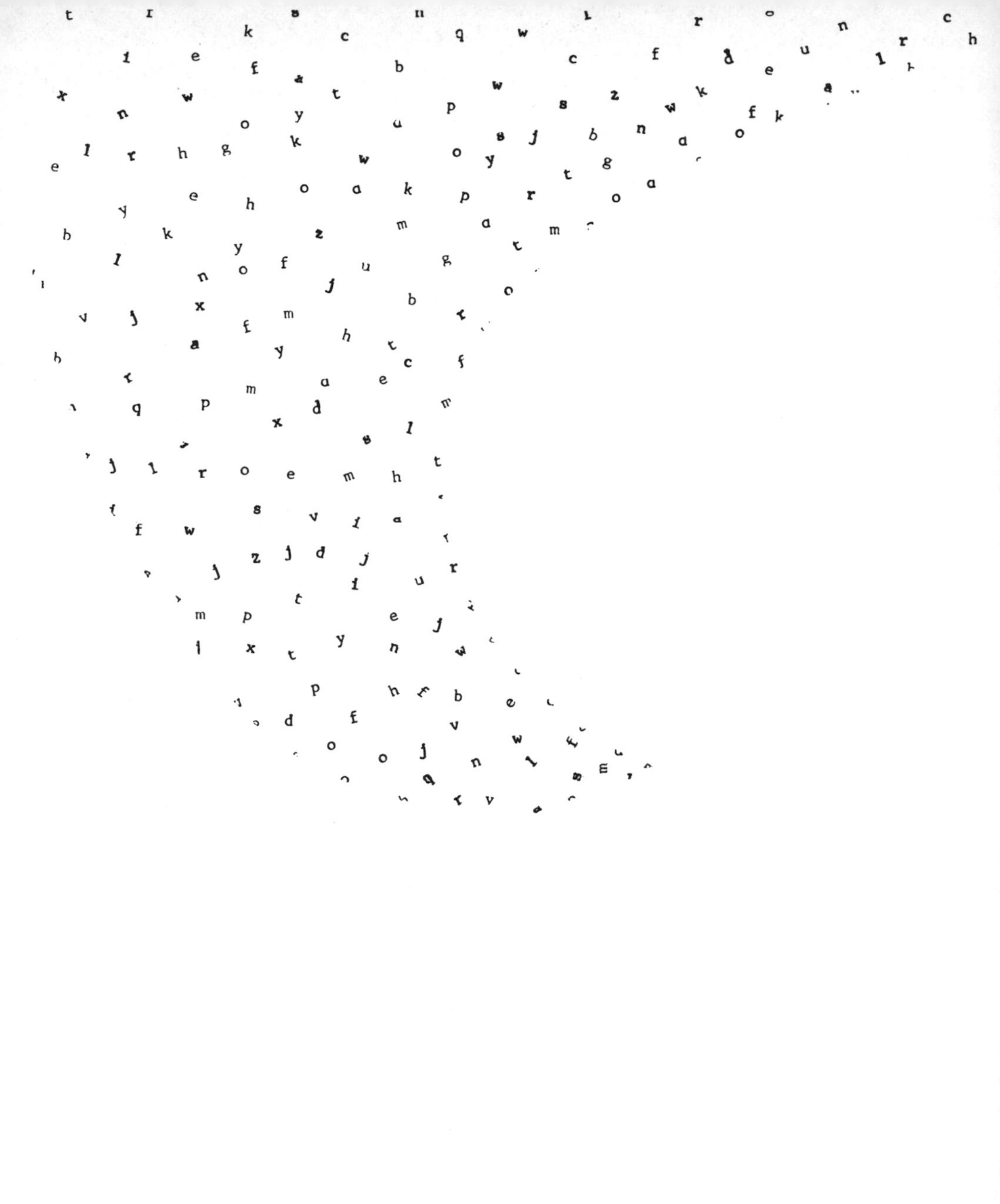

process '76

sun thru the window clouds static over a countryside of snow. feel my way along hills & soft mounds my nephew derek laughs as he (bundled up warm) plunges in & out of snow he loves the toboggan ride squeals with delight each time

back in my place i see cold nights in autumn pass quickly into snow moved here in september from another scene from many people to just- me 'i'll save up enuff money' i said '& try it for a year or so' new phase of the journey pass it on to you i hesitate before plunging in cool bath of language flows onto the page

i sit by the keyboard snow falls each flake a distinct sign among countless shows how primitive our alphabet is fragments & arrangements snow & wind wind blows over hills my balcony these days seasons change from red to green & back again each day a different world each world a different day we move thru shadows our eyes see it is the light blinds us shadows we feel within i raise my hands let them fall upon the waiting letters & begin those roads i remember those long roads my father & i would walk along (trying to fill in the emptiness) stop & examine rocks stoop & spy among the leaves walk deeper into the forest 'it is time' he wd say 'it is time it is time' & then i wd lose him somewhere ahead of me he wd vanish into only a dream i wake up in a room somewhere in the future there is no future don juan says only now for the warrior we shud all be warri

when the streets ran thru with water teddy & i played in spring in his backyard spongy earth always wet with peat moss & twigs the earth revolves we grow older & learn to love or not it is their time our time the next time lordy lordy not enuff time here i complain abt it & at the same time waste it oh well i get things done anyway quite a bit actually (its piling up) makes me feel younger reversal of the process of aging at 34 retracing my steps searching backwards ever farther into that singular history that i am

mother a farm girl raised in a german village west of kitchener born in february as were paul & dad her mother rebecca hahn mother of 4 girls dad met her one evening at the wonderland ballroom london ontario where both he & i were born & they danced into one anothers lives here i am years later writing about them writing about them lord lord it is a strange strange world in which we live in which we do ma & she moved to london to work for remington till she met pa circa 1935 the only job she ever h from the time i came on on a 'housewife' withdrew from the workaday world i cant reall blame her for that if only she cudve found something to do... once told alfie she reminded me of a small (tho she is not a small woman) nervous bird with frightened eyes

pa? bummed around a bit i think worked he sd 'packing crates in sudbury had a littl room in the sudbury hotel it was the lonliest period of my life' i guess he decided to ge married then worked for toledo scales now years later he has a workshop full of toys ve successfull business very creative man did it all on his own but you can see the missing parts the parts where love did not have its full say happens to most of us today

his mother maddie & father sam lived in london once was farmland right out behind the house...shows you how much the city has grown... sam was a streetcar conductor turn of the century three generations ago used to drive right past the house 508 central ave... sam

so there it is we grow & change now we live elsewhere in other rooms other citie some of us folks we dont have drift abt continents some of us too many folks the tide turns fills & empties us rooms about the earth shadows & lights of passing days

You can't be telling me about me this way.

how successful was it? hmm cant really say i know it started out well enough both of us were quite quiet at first paid little attention to either the text or extra-textial facets of our lives no daily i went about my business sought out contacts at the office or elsewhere engaged in (at least what i thot at the time were) constructive conversations...

the words themselves seemed to come without any effort no it was not the wordflow that was the problem we relate back to the line & see espacial contours within more or less singular the part of the day i remember (where we were then) down by the lake the crystal water rushing in cataracts falling waves splitting over rocks & wrinkled pier we mustve walked for miles thru sand stopping only intermittently we said little fortunately had come out far enough to leave the city behind steps tracing into underbrush leaves heaving in wind lay on our backs for a while watching clouds followed for a long time the outline of a truncated forest searched thru a giant mushroom patch found an answer hung on a limb

of course there were many days i expect could have passed just as happily actually this way (that is the way this is) i have little regrets sit & think ahead

looked his way, but sd 0.

— but its true! he sd, looking about him, from one face to another. hes been following me, I tell you. For days now. & i dont know why. I cant get him to talk! He looked into the face of the man standing before him: the man sd: 'sign out a warrant for him then. But I dont know his name, he wont tell me. The car rumbled along thru the tunnel, quietly. Now everyone in the car was looking at him. 5 had gathered round the scene, their eyes on him, watching. What if someone recognized him? He backed away. The train finally pulled in to O-G station, gratefully, he got out. He walked the richard & i talked yesterday of starting a small press we dubbed 'phenomenon press' we both have enough material we figure to put out three or four issues of our work alone that wont be the idea of course there are so many people we know with such new & exciting things to offer who simply have no outlet our first issue we decided will be modest enough a 10 page piece from each of us & future issues hugo ball stein a concrete anthology mccaffery bp narrative/comix could go on no lack of ideas for sure! had talked of ths before actually but now seems the right time & we talked of what else was new richard working on a sci-fi piece & me finishing the 1st novel that likely will never be read "shit" written on 167 sheets of toilet tissue (to be used as read) trying to take the wrinkles out of some old material fun going back/smoothing it all out

over this last month or two began to realize the importance of research is so exciting to see what others are doing stimulates my own creative impulses "yeah man i cd do this with that... that with this..." that is a hell of a gas! readings for april pound fry cage in march olson zukofsky triquarterly 37 barths s/z

& then there is the apocalypsis each monday night for the performance in october at st pauls steve mccaffery guides us is quite a fellow quite a fellow reading again thru dr sadhus muffins is beautiful 'a book of written readings' leanings in new directions

on the edge of april may peeking in white sleep over waking begins earth moves is good to be alive to see it thru a part of it

wake up early spend hours on my balcony drunk on green & yellow days / black & yellow nights linda wants to go camping at sauble beach on the 24th as we did last year weather was just bareably warm kept the fire going for a long time that first night took a trip to the beach next day all the vans rolling homes must be great to see the country that way that afternoon walked thru a pine forest behind our campsite brown pinebed floor absorbs the sound reminds me of the stillness the silence within a cathedral pine roof sun thru stained glass as thru walls of pine birds call back & forth echo their delight perhaps the lords true church

return trip along the 401 slide into the city from the north structured homes & structured dreams themes change spring opens finally i sit on my porch stare into leaves & sky from nature we learn to continue nights the sky fills barrie how often i remember your words "none of this made sense till i looked up
raised my head above the earth to study heaven"

sit in my flat writing lamps heavy yellow light floods the room words flow onto the page i merely transmit them thru the years

sun stored for another day / dream all night / chase the moon away

my lady comes to me love on a caring scale hours we find our own too precious to leave behind still love you i still do & not yet halfway thru

work opening up starting 2nd book of tales (as this is) is my way where i live there are other ways outside i am not in we grant one another poems it is in the language it is in the air so much everywhere so much we miss of mystery goes by john & i have dinner on the porch he is going to moosonee to supervise a building project in the fall a building project for the metis who may not even want it! tells me later it is hard to know who to speak or how to up there it is cold he says it is cold ice blue sky all day no change in weather or landscape worked for three months before anyone spoke to him the manager said 'that's pretty good usually takes abt five' but he looked good anyway in his new suit & the climate suits him a whole different culture

lasagna & wine on the porch mild breezes trees full bloom a FOREST in my backyard! the cats love it out here as much as i do keep their eyes on the pigeons have an image of him plodding thru night black horizon ahead dazzling moonlit snow walking forever again & again to somewhere just beyond here

lay in bed sleeping a dream where areas look for an exit it is night it is not my turn not my fault turn right & am back eons ago hunting a lost bear turns hurriedly away i am beside him running too wake up it is 4 oclock go out onto the porch sit for an hour the sky lightens steadily by degrees now that is reality!

walked down to the store today for some fruit met sylvia on the way beautiful lady i see you in a dream as well we are all there your hands & mine touch/speak daily hold out hope as a shining star

the trees sway gently today is monday work going well what more could i ask for? by degrees body wakens it is fall where i am elsewhere (so they say) it is spring

i finally lay aside my lifelong disguise these evenings i sit on the porch think it clear think it beautiful always try to be home before the sun sets to watch the trees dark & darken their black fingers resting in a red sky smitty has always been a special fellow for me when we meet these days is special even more an easiness we had to struggle for he & owen sound going to amsterdam thursday to participate in the ninth international sound poetry festival first time hes been abroad hopes to see something of england & scotland too bon aventure! we had lunch yesterday noon at vivaxis

mid july work going well have completed three new pieces this month i find this country a rewarding place to be have the freedom to write & move when & if i wish money is not the problem day to day living is the people i know reflect their energies in what they paint write etcetera at the end of her book 'survival' margaret atwood asks the q what happens after survival ok well why not be noted for our positive attitude towards life from now on (what have we really got to complain abt?) anyway i find that friends make all the difference in the world like ALL the difference you write/live in a vacuume/ you live/write in a vacuume or choose to work against that self-involvement

finally got the writing desk i wanted searched for that desk for two months! needed one less than 38" wide to fit into the nook by the window found one 37½" gorgeous fine finish four large drawers was ready to give up when i found it the store wasnt open but i wanted it so bad i just sat on it waited there for three hours till the shopkeeper came along "i was going to sell it for $65 (he sd) but for you $60" i wd have paid $80 for it easy my colours brown orange yellow

i am my fingers are this page i am working on right now abt lower right side of which you are in to too i shall tell you a tale of suspense suspended... at just that moment the duke walked along the southern edge of town the marshall closed in on him from the east 'hold it duke' he sd 'your killin days are over' the duke turned slowly smiled 'not for long marshall not for long...' the marshall heard the safetys click on a pair of 45s behind him where the hell was that deputy when you needed him sun falls thru the edge of the desert lands squarely in my eyes

smitty munches on his salad i am back in yesterday noon he leaves for amsterdam thursday bon aventure!

voices keep speaking   i dont know what to do

all these words   to write thru

so far to go   only so much time to spend

lord how will i get there   how will it end

my typewriter humms   have lunch at the zum today with pat

decorate my flat this afternoon   paint furniture   white fingers closing over a brush

"must paint a picture for that space on the wall"   each segment requires   a personal touch   you live where you make

those ready made homes   food   shit   "we're all stuffed to death   look at that man wandering the street   alcoholic in midday   looking for a tree to lie under, to sleep it off"   the tonal gone, don juan wd say   nothing but a shell/to fill with alcohol   green shutes of youth   destroyed

"where are you?"

"here"

"where are you now?"

"over here in this box   a cozy coffin   mother made for me"

buried in yesterdays dreams ... of yesterdays

finished 2nd deck last week   the hardest of the 4   took 6 weeks   the 1st & 3rd took only 2   the fourth 4

there are days when the weather just doesnt register

"come in..."

research going well   (where shall i drop this space?)   a record writ   of which a few i include here   why dont we all do it don juan says   we are streaming & sure enough most of us can see the stars   it is energy it is heat

it is near the end of august now   i am green   & warm   & all right now

green   & warm   & all right now

warm   & all right now

all right now

incredibly spicey tale, if you get what I mean — that is, if you go in for that sort of thing. [a yawning] I particularly like, as well, the images of [illegible] exquisite [illegible] from the story. This is an exact quote from the tale! exciting, eh!

ha ha ha. well, all frivolity aside folks, the tale actually is quite serious. It is a quite [illegible] [illegible] by Miss Islandia when she discovers ~~Randy Kemph~~ Phillipe is not a homosexual after all!!) moody, yet straightforward, shadowy, yet clean; unfortunate, yet vague.

Before ~~beginning, though, a word of appreciation~~ ~~Well ladies & gentlemen, I may, I really should~~ [illegible]

~~Before ending, however,~~ I should just like to acknowledge my appreciation to Miss Whistheim who so knowingly, yet so unself-consciously type, & retyped the story ~~to my standards of perfection~~ without a whimper of protest ~~without a word of~~ sugg'n [illegible] the serious flaws in it [illegible] (regrettably especially), so [illegible] Prof Sakhtikla [illegible] ~~alcoholic & embroider~~ (this comes out in the story, actually) For this sugg'n I might alter certain facts concerning the ~~embarrassing~~ [illegible] activities of one of the main characters. But upon my ~~I have~~ kindly refused. notice Prof Sakhtikla is not here with us tonight. ~~Most unfortunate~~! [cannot be] indicated his long-overdue desire to travel & so, regretfully, i am painting a picture

picture of a sunflower   i have painted a room for my wall   a picture 3' x 4'   green acrylic applied with a pestle (no brushes) abt ¼" thick then the (yellow) flower halfway down towards the left   just built the paint out & out & out   did it until it was right added some wood chips to the top   thot of adding some sand but didnt   would have liked to add water- not blue paint- water!   love to have a picture i cud water   couldnt figure out how tho

i speak out into this turbulence called living   you have outguessed me again   it is not true   it is not false   sometimes when you come i am in   sometimes when you come i am not in   vancouver in september for a tour   thot id never hear those words spoken   finally met billy   west coast air   in the mountains wanted to run off like the lane brothers   just get the hell lost up there   in all those trees   mountains & sky   stood for a long time in the redwood forest   shaking as it rained   the thot that those trees over 2000 years old   were living when the roman empire was   long before america etcetera   you could take all of america out of that time span & not even miss it even now no way it can exist as it is for even another hundred years   those trees will still be there then   i hope   facing the sun

as there is no life in our solar system so advanced as on earth   those trees are the oldest living creatures within a minimum range of 4.3 light years or 25 284 000 000 000 miles   the distance to alpha centauri   if life is considered precious   then those trees among the most precious creatures upon the earth should be given every consideration   we show our ignorance   our lack of civilization   by carving <u>holes</u> thru them for <u>cars</u>!!

took the train back across canada   what can i say so many have said it   no matter which part of the world you live in   she is a blue blue lady gowned in greens & browns   soft fair/sunlight hair   how lucky we are   she remains so tolerant   so far

is early october first signs of cold traces among trees
sky turns these days as if it knows had a talk with bp this morning at the book
"how are the cards coming?" he sd "fine" i sd he digs them drop down to the oyster bar
see the link hes getting tired of playing there hope he gets this gig at shakespeares
hed thrive there so comings & goings...

seems nothing much tho always in the background the sets continue to unfold new possibilities revealed each day new plays to enter in to been reading biographies this last month stein russell simone de beauvoir sartre's 'les mots' a fascinating original piece of writing he has such a joy around using & playing with words fascinating what people have done with their lives oh lord the love for craft should drive us to engagement not to suicide!!

can see the day when artists will be leaders in the world not lawyers or philosophers imagine a future where the priority is art (perhaps with a capital "a"?) mans <u>true</u> playground once we've found a way to make machines do our work for us is the only logical choice we've tried everything else

oh i wish i were there i could receive a postcard from tomorrow just a few lines to see what it would be like there to see tomorrow we must let the earth reclaim us not abuse her furthur in killing her we kill ourselves therei lay her ultimate claim upon us

They rented a room in a Mrs. Jones, on the 1st floor, who was an alcoholic. [illegible] as he planned, happily living on [illegible] the rent payments being sufficient to still this curiosity. Mrs. Jones was in his mind thinking although he had been thinking for some time, appeared to be about mid-forty. So far as J S knew, he had no friends, & indeed, Mrs J. preferred it that way. All the same, he was a friend of people, although [illegible] brain continuously threatening storm.

He didn't care. He was a cold one, one that is in which death appealed to him more than life. Get it on with. Get it over with. 'Let the storm come,' he might have said, 'it will be a longed-for relief to finally have it at an end.' & so, he lived a form of suicide, [illegible] storm [illegible] to think things at least but some someone allotting him for a time a magical world, where things were & what they were, when the storm subsided into a honey-like ~~musical~~ calm, & things were fine — [illegible] Of course, he thereby [illegible] less & less. But of course, in concert with drinking, his ability to fight the storm, his hopes for survival upon a stormy sea, his outlook onto the world in which he existed, his hope for his manhood, his estimation of himself, receded more & more.

It seemed a circle only death could resolve, — but then, for all cold ones, this is the primary sin.

daily schedule get up abt 9 work till noon walk down to the zum (the office) or roy rogers or woolworths have a coffee see whos there do some light revisions perhaps a bit of reading walk back to the y perhaps run a bit take a swim a shower go home have some lunch- its abt 3-4 oclock by then- an hour nap usually leave the evenings open for socializing last night peter mac was over hes going to take a year off & do some writing same as me he has several things in mind i think hes a bit frightened of it tho i hope that passes & it becomes as exciting for him as it has been (is) for me going to see ben wolfitt tonight we are going to try a collaborative piece which should be interesting also i want to ask him if he can do illustrations i have an idea for a cartoon strip

this afternoon i make the rounds large flakes falling in reasonably warm air (for this time of year) lord i do wish for spring/summer! i miss it already tho winter has only begun occasionally stop in at robarts library scan the periodicals tri quarterly review encounter open letter psychology & the arts etcetera well what can one do? complain &/or work towards it- i choose &

changed my diet considerably bot a steamer last month steamed vegetables quite tasty i think at last i'll be able to get off the gorp food plan my weekly menus around fish vegetables chicken soups & salads- with the occasional pizza thrown in

since i do mostly headwork the y is good for me too alfie says yeah but you should do things with people too / your biggest problem has always been to get out of yourself what can i do but listen to him he is a guide leads me thru unexplored regions shud i chose to follow perhaps a bit too simplistic but then i prefer metaphor to reason sometime during our journey i shall say to him 'that is far enough / i've got the picture now you need accompany me no furthur / i'll take it from here...' don juan says a warrior is ready each & every moment to fight with his death & i think of reichs quote from the bible in 'the murder of christ' "Watch therefore, for you know neither the day nor the hour"

thot i'd forget you did you   no   those old carpets   the stairs   the cold glass
windows   no no i know   it is time for a change   energy rises to the surface   it is the
lonliness gets you   must be a compromise somewhere between life on your own & a totally
social existence   need that time & space to think for yourself   otherwise go crazy
happened to a friend of mine   likely happened to a friend of yours too   forget abt myself
sometimes   well i guess perhaps i'd like to move into a house somewhere   a home   at least
somewhere with friends   what i'd really like is a place by the sea   nothing fancy   just a
place by the sea   sound & motion of waves roll in   so beautiful   steins repitition   an
insistence within speaks to you   each wave (breath) difft yet similar   ice blue eyes
clouds floating in water sky   where were you when i dreamed you existed & now i am awake
where   sometimes it rains out here   i get cold & wet   it is different now from when our
fathers came   yet similar   pick up a shell from the beach today   it whispers to me to list
this evening wrapping gifts to take home   gifts   to bring with me   gifts   to give to
friends   xmas brings out the santa claus in me   always like to make things for people
if i only have time to make a card   that xmas at 316 i made over 20 gifts -- each of them quite
different   really funny because i was angry & wouldnt speak to anyone while i worked on their
gifts   no   the gifts turned out fine   christmas & the snow flies   lands lightly on your
collar   warm fur coats   smiles the ladies wear   time of remembering the lights the eastern
star been there 2000 years   on the xmas tree we try to imitate
tyr to make it like the one before the one before the one before   as if
try to pick the best from past experience   is what art is
oh yes   it is names i give you   voices i recall   old old winters ago on grandmas
farm   old wood the pine fire crackling   heat & sparks rising thru the grate   sometime
even before electricity   how out of place it looked   grandpa was reluctant to use it
preferred candles   perhaps he was right
a pretty dress for her daughter   my mother   father sits by the side beaming   the way it
was?   the way it might have been   yes & no   i play with a small toy in the centre of
the room   examine it   unfold it   then i saw the world as a bright happy place   just
beginning to get back to that again the childlike joy we all knew/most of us lose
folding these threads together   wrapping them about one another   in & out
finally unfolding from the frames   something new is made   its you i'm talking to   a gift
from me to you

Pope Leo: El Elope
A TRAGEDY IN FOUR LETTERS
FILE
POP ELO
POPE LEO
ART:

O LO
POPE LEO
ELOPE!

O POPE LEO! PEOPLE POLL PEOPLE! PEOPLE POLE PEOPLE! LO PEOPLE!
PEEL, POLE PEOPLE, O PEEP LEEP, EEL PEOPLE, LOP PEOPLE, LOLL, POOL LOOP-PLOP! POLO PEP-POOP!
OLE!!

PEOPLE? PEOPLE! O! LO! POP ELO, POPE ELOPE POOL POLL...
PEOPLE LOLL! OLE!
LO! POP ELO LOOP POPE POOL POLL!

LEEEEOOOOOOOOO
OOO...
ELO ELOPE...
ELO LOOP POPE...
POOL, PEEL POLL...
LEEP! ELO, LEEP!
POP ELO PEEL POPE LEO;
PEEL LO PEOPLE,
LOLL, LO.
FINIS

The Difference

ractioncontractionc
ractioncontractioncontracti
tractioncontractioncontractioncon
ractioncontractioncontractioncontract
oncontractioncontractioncontractioncontrac
tractioncontractioncontractioncontractioncont
ractioncontractiANSIONEXPANSIOcontractioncontrac
ioncontractioncSIONEXPANSIONEXPANoncontractioncon
ntractioncontSIONEXPANSIONEXPANSIONactioncontracti
actioncontracIONEXPANSIONEXPANSIONEXPANcontractioncon
ontractionconONEXPANSIONEXPANSIONEXPANSIOoncontraction
actioncontraPANSIONEXPANSIONEXPANSIONEXPANtractioncontr
oncontractioSIONEXPANSIONEXPANSIONEXPANSIONtioncontracti
ntractionconXPANSIONEXPANSIONEXPANSIONEXPANcontractionco
actioncontrNSIONEXPANSIONEXPANSIONEXPANSIOtractioncontr
ntractionconXPANSIONEXPANSIONEXPANSIONEXPANcontractionco
ctioncontracSIONEXPANSIONEXPANSIONEXPANSIOractioncontra
ntractionconANSIONEXPANSIONEXPANSIONEXPAoncontraction
actioncontracPANSIONEXPANSIONEXPANSIONEcontractioncor
ntractioncontIONEXPANSIONEXPANSIONEactioncontracti
ctioncontractioIONEXPANSIONEXPANctioncontraction
tractioncontractioANSIONEXPioncontractioncontra
tractioncontractioncontractioncontractioncon
ntractioncontractioncontractioncontractio
ntractioncontractioncontractioncontrac
ntractioncontractioncontractionco
ontractioncontractioncontra
ntractioncontractio

NTRACTIONCONTR

TRACTIONCONTRACTIONCONTR

NTRACTIONCONTRACTIONCONTRACTIO

TRACTIONCONTRACTIONCONTRACTIONCONTRA

CTIONCONTRACTIONCONTRACTIONCONTRACTIONCO

NTRACTIONCONTRACTIONCONTRACTIONCONTRACTIONC

TRACTIONCONTRACTIONCONTRACTIONCONTRACTIONCONTR

TIONCONTRACTIONCONTRACTEXPANSCONTRACTIONCONTRACTIONC

NTRACTIONCONTRACTIONCONTRACTIONCONTRACTIONCONTRACT

CTIONCONTRACTIONCONTRACTIONCONTRACTIONCONTRACTIONCON

ACTIONCONTRACTIONCONTRANSionexpansionCONTRACTIONCONT

NTRACTIONCONTRACTIONConexpansionexPTRACTIONCONTRACTIONC

TIONCONTRACTIONCONTonexpansionexpansIONCONTRACTIONCONTRAC

NTRACTIONCONTRACTIONexpansionexpansionCTIONCONTRACTIONCON

TIONCONTRACTIONCONionexpansionexpansCONTRACTIONCONTRAC

NTRACTIONCONTRACTIsionexpansionexpanACTIONCONTRACTIONCO

NCONTRACTIONCONTRAexpansionexpansionNTRACTIONCONTRACTIO

RACTIONCONTRACTIONCexpansionexpansIONCONTRACTIONCONT

NTRACTIONCONTRACTIONConexpansionCONTRACTIONCONTRACTION

CTIONCONTRACTIONCONTRACTIONCONTRACTIONCONTRACTIONCONT

CONTRACTIONCONTRACTIONCONTRACTIONCONTRACTIONCONTRAC

RACTIONCONTRACTIONCONTRACTIONCONTRACTIONCONTRACTI

NTRACTIONCONTRACTIONCONTRACTIONCONTRACTIONCONT

TIONCONTRACTIONCONTRACTIONCONTRACTIONCONTRA

NTRACTIONCONTRACTIONCONTRACTIONCONTRACT

NCONTRACTIONCONTRACTIONCONTRACTIONCO

CTIONCONTRACTIONCONTRACTIONCONT

TRACTIONCONTRACTIONCONTR

NTRACTIONCONT

..actioncontra..
..ractioncontractioncontr..
..ractioncontractioncontraction..
..actioncontractioncontractioncontrac
cioncontractioncont..ONE..contractioncon..
..ntractioncontr..EXPANS..ONEXPANSI..contractionc
..ractioncon..IONEX..IONEXPANS..ctioncontr..
..tioncont..EXPANSIONEXPANS..ONEXPANSION..ontractio..
..ontract..ONEXPANSIONEXPANSIONEXPA..SIONEX..contrac..
..ncontract..PANSIONEXPANSIONEXPANSIONEXPANS..oncontra..
actioncont..EXPANSIONEXPANSIONEXPANSIONE..actioncon
ontractio..EXPANSIONEXPANSIONEXPANSIONEXPA..contraction..
ctioncont..ONEXPANSIONEXPANSIONEXPANSIONEXP..ONI..ioncontr
..ontract..PANSIONEXPANSIONEXPANSIONEXPANSIONEXPA..ntracti..
..raction..NEXPANSIONEXPANSIONEXPANSIONEXPANSIONEX..raction
oncontrac..PANSIONEXPANSIONEXPANSIONEXPANSIONEX..cont
contracti..NEXPANSIONEXPANSIONEXPANSIONEXP..action
ctioncont..EXPANSIONEXPANSIONEXPANSIONEXPA..ractio..
..ontractio..EXPANSIONEXPANSIONEXPANSIONEXPANS..ctionc
..ractioncon..PANS..NEXPANSIONEXPANSION..PANSIO..oncontra..
ioncontrac..IONEX..IONEXPANSIONEXPANS..ONEX..actioncont
ontractioncon..PANS..IONEX..PANS ONEX..actioncon..
..actioncontra..ioncontrac..
ontractio.. ONEXPANS..ONEXPA..contractionc
..ontractio.. ..ractioncontractioncontrac..
..ontractio..contractioncontractioncon..
..ontractioncontractioncontractio..
..contractioncontractioncon..
..tioncontractio..

ACTIONCON

IONCONTRACTIONCON

NTRACTIONCONTRACTIONCO

IONCONTRACTIONCONTRACTION

NTRACTIONCONTRACTIONCONTRACT

ACTIONCONTRACTIONCONTRACTIONCON

TRACTIONCONTRACTIONCONTRACTIONC

TIONCONTRACTIONCONTRACTIONCONTRAC

NTRACTIONCONTRACTIONCONTRACTIONCO

IONCONTRACTIONCONTRACTIONCONTRACT

TIONCONTRACTIONCONTRACTIONCONTR

NTRACTIONCONTRACTIONCONTRACTIC

CTIONCONTRACTIONCONTRACTIONCO

NTRACTIONCONTRACTIONCONTRA

NTRACTIONCONTRACTIONCO

ACTIONCONTRACTIONCO

ONTRACTIONC

actionc ntracti ontracti contrac

ontractioncoNEXPANS EXPANS ntract

ractioncontractioncon IONEXPANS ioncon

ioncont IONEXPANS IONEXPANS IONEX ractic

ontraction PANS IONEXPANS ION ntra

ctioncon PANS IONEXPANS IONEXPA ncont

ntraction PANS IONEXPANS IONEXPANS IONEX contr

ctioncon ONEXPANS IONEXPANS IONEXPANS IO contract

ntrac SIONEXPANS IONEXPANS IONEXPANS IONEXPA ctioncon

PANS IONEXPANS IONEXPANS IONEXPANS ntra

XPANS IONEXPANS IONEXPANS IONEXPANS ncon

SIONEXPANS IONEXPANS IONEXPANS IONE ctio

IONEXPANS IONEXPANS IONEXPANS IONEX ontract

NSIONEXPANS IONEXPANS IONEXPANS IONEXPANS tioncon

IONEXPANS IONEXPANS IONEXPANS IONEXPANS ontracti

PANS IONEXPANS IONEXPANS IONEXPA ioncontrac

IONEXPANS IONEXPANS IONEXPANS

actio IONEXPANS IONEXPANS IONEXPANS IONE

ntraction NSIONEXPANS IONEXPANS IONEXPANS IONE contract

ctioncon IONEXPANS ioncontra

contr ioncontrac contra

ction ontr actioncc

contrac ioncont

ctioncon racti

ontractio ionc

contractioncont

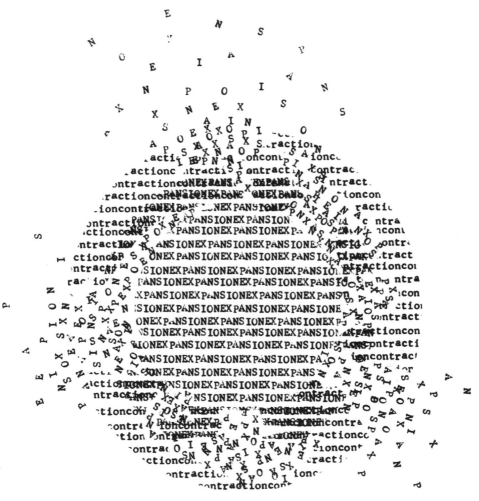

[illegible]
RACTIONCONTRA
IONCONTRACTIONCONT
ONTRACTIONCONTRACTION
TRACTIONCONTRACTIONCONT
CONTRACTIONCONTRACTIONCON
IONCONTRACTIONCONTRACTIO
RACTIONCONTRACTIONCONTRA
CONTRACTIONCONTRACTIONC
CTIONCONTRACTIONCONTRA
TIONCONTRACTIONCONT
CONTRACTIONCONT
IONCONT

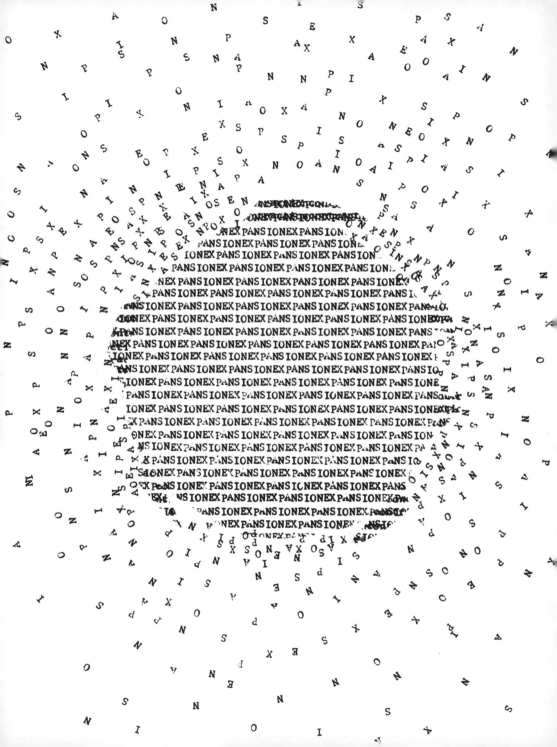

IONEX PANS IONEX PANS IONE
PANS IONEX PANS IONEX PANS IONE
IONEX PANS IONEX PANS IONEX PANS ION
PANS IONEX PANS IONEX PANS IONEX PANS ION
NEX PANS IONEX PANS IONEX PANS IONEX PANS IONEX
PANS IONEX PANS IONEX PANS IONEX PANS IONEX PANS I
PANS IONEX PANS IONEX PANS IONEX PANS IONEX PANS
IONEX PANS IONEX PANS IONEX PANS IONEX PANS IONEX
PANS IONEX PANS IONEX PANS IONEX PANS IONEX PANS
NEX PANS IONEX PANS IONEX PANS IONEX PANS IONEX PA
IONEX PANS IONEX PANS IONEX PANS IONEX PANS IONEX
PANS IONEX PANS IONEX PANS IONEX PANS IONEX PANS IO
IONEX PANS IONEX PANS IONEX PANS IONEX PANS IONE
PANS IONEX PANS IONEX PANS IONEX PANS IONEX PANS
IONEX PANS IONEX PANS IONEX PANS IONEX PANS IONEX
EX PANS IONEX PANS IONEX PANS IONEX PANS IONEX PA
ONEX PANS IONEX PANS IONEX PANS IONEX PANS ION
NS IONEX PANS IONEX PANS IONEX PANS IONEX PANS IONEX PA
X PANS IONEX PANS IONEX PANS IONEX PANS IONEX PANS IO
IONEX PANS IONEX PANS IONEX PANS IONEX PANS IONEX
X PANS IONEX PANS IONEX PANS IONEX PANS IONEX PANS
NS IONEX PANS IONEX PANS IONEX PANS IONEX
PANS IONEX PANS IONEX PANS IONEX
NEX PANS IONEX PANS IONEX

ONTRACT
RACTION
IONCONT

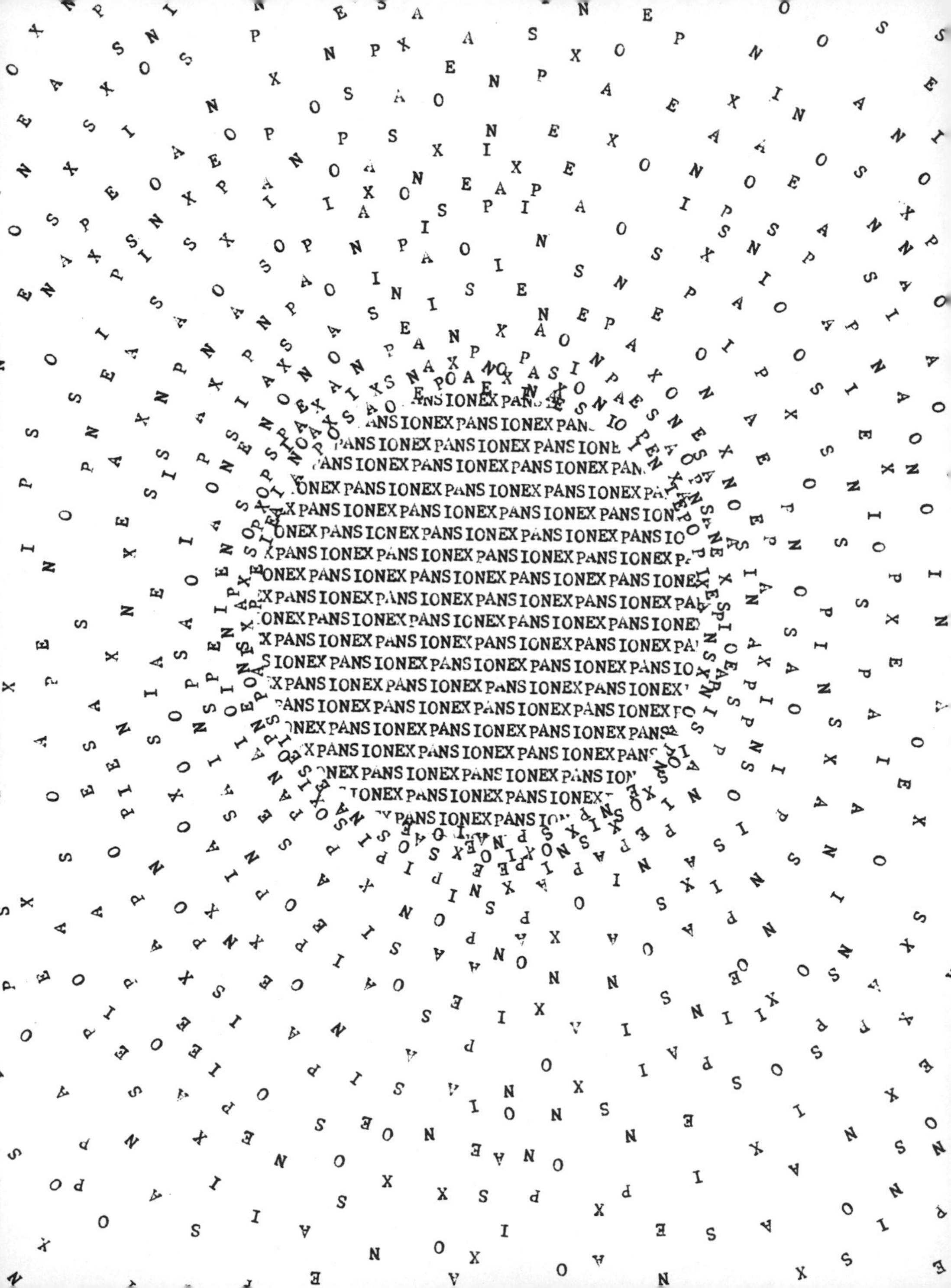

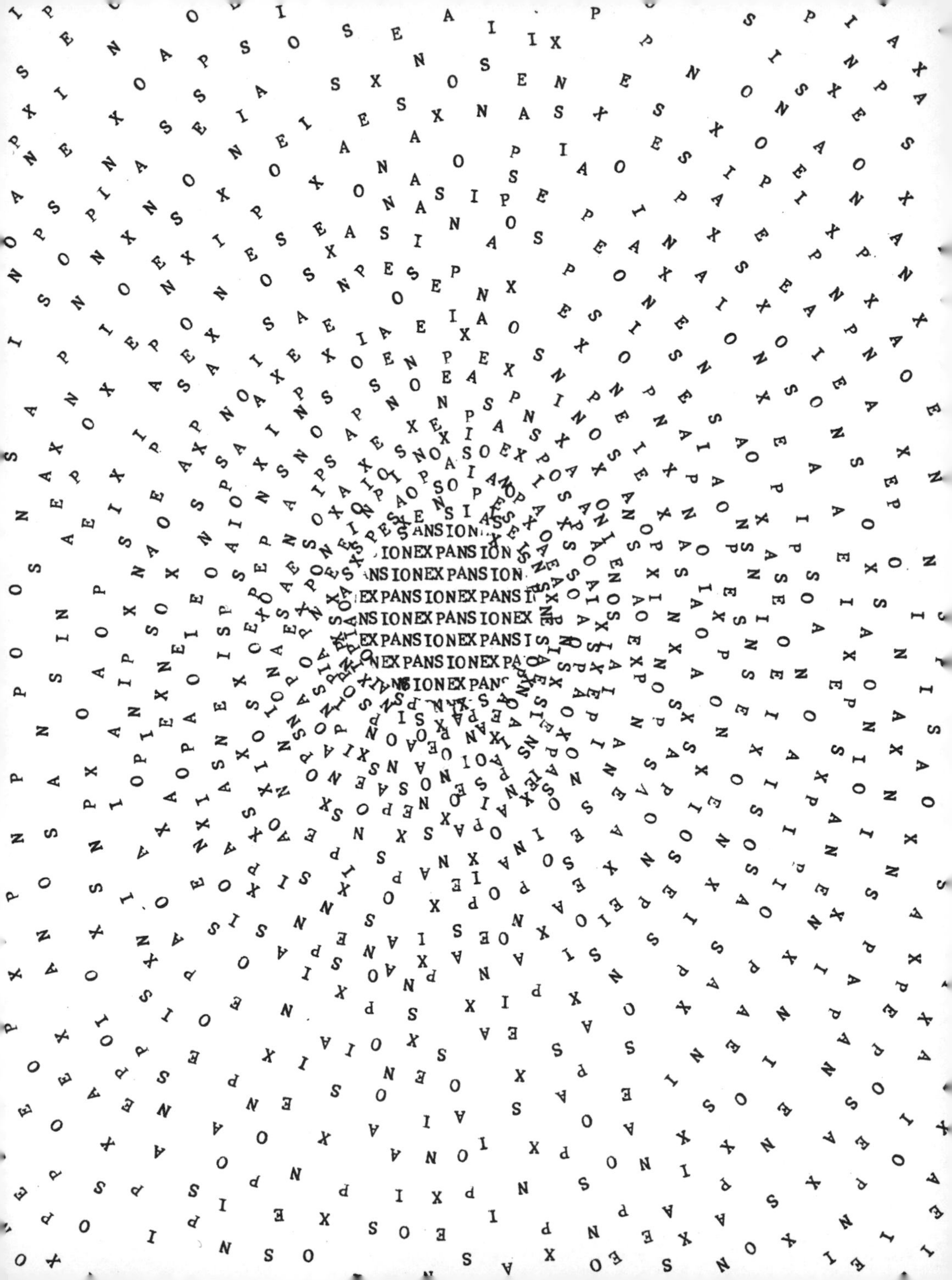

The Ramp

1.

THE GREAT TRANSCONTINENTAL HIGHWAY, designed and built by the Architect Ramos, was completed near the end of the second millenium. It invariably emerged as the central feature in any of the then-contemporary surveys of travel routes, and being the largest, most complex roadway ever designed by man, it was only natural that this should be so. Yet even that multilane, coast-to-coast route had its rivals. The North-South Freeway (for example) extended farther each year, both into the Northland where (it was rumoured) rich resources lay beneath the snow; and into tropical Southern climes, which doubtless contained mystery and adventure enough to lure a variety of speculators and treasure-seekers. And of course there was the Great Junction, the intersection of these two routes in the Central Midwest. Any survey would have to allot a significant section for its description, including a number of explanatory maps, as the Great Junction was a seven-tiered system of cloverleaves which rose 2.82 kilometers above ground level, and was 213.6 kilometers in diameter. It was built under the supervision of Ramos by a Task Force of analysts, mathematicians, and physicists, and was said by all to be a masterpiece of modern architectural engineering, surely one of the finest achievements of modern man.

As well, any survey would mention such routes as the West Lake Interchange, a system of roads, viaducts, and tunnels which interconnected thousands of Western islands, fed roadways down into island streets and towns which had come to be known as 'residential sectors,' for they housed millions of the inhabitants in that part of the world. The large roadways to the South, a variety of expressways, freeways, biways, etc., each with their own particular feel, or 'character,' if you like – could as well be noted, all attesting to the belief then held by practitioners and devotees that, since a natural aesthetic was both involved and anticipated, roadbuilding was an art form, rather than simply a contemporary necessity. Indeed, the roadbuilders manipulated the driver's environment, attempted to present him with an entertaining landscape, one calculated to keep him interested, alert; it had long been established that a boring roadway caused drowsiness, lack of concentration, and, as a result, accidents.

YET the writers of such booklets often fail to mention the indigenous development of ramp systems, likely considering them to be a minor aspect of the roadbuilders' problems, and in any case not half so interesting as the finished product, the great roadways themselves. The contrary, however, is the case: the great roadways posed neither theoretical nor practical problems for Ramos and his men; no, it was the underlying mesh, the cobweblike support systems of the more dexterous roadways which had to be worked and reworked theoretically, reprogrammed time and again. Like the stresses and strains undergone in the

War Games of days of old, the great builders would arrange and rearrange routes and counterroutes, study the pros and cons of each, hold conferences, dispute and compute for months — perhaps years — before arriving at a decision as to how a particular ramp system should be structured, sloped, out of what material it should be made, how many lanes, and so on.

And these ramps ran everywhere: indiscriminate, they spanned the mansions of the rich, the huts of the poor; variable, some ran a few metres, others kilometres, in single or multilane breadths, above, on, or underground. Some entered remote regions of the world indeed: pavement rolled through dark, forbidding jungles; smooth causeways effectively levelled coastal mountain ranges; pillars towered up from southern swamplands, the stolid shadows of their roadways falling obtrusively upon the life-cycles taking place beneath.

A few scholars considered it possible that some ramps might extend through areas where ancient civilizations still flourished — perhaps proffering a culture superior to ours; others scoffed at such a foolish notion, reminding such dreamers that the world had long since been settled, that no such culture could possibly have gone undetected. But whatever the case, these ramps ran anywhere, in any shape or size necessary to facilitate the pursuit of commerce in the modern industrial state.

IT MIGHT AS WELL BE MENTIONED that the roadways offered a variety of occupations for many. An army of bureaucrats and trained professional men was required to keep statistical and financial accounts, personnel records; traffic controllers, analysts, and programmers were kept busy doing time-study charts, traffic counts, recommending improvements — even closures — of various roadways. These men and women — the bureaucratic elite — worked side by side with the roadbuilders, who had become the highest paid, most respected professionals in the world. It was considered a privilege to work with them, a privilege strongly competed for in universities across the land.

The blue collar force (all employed by the Department of Roads) consisted of (1) roadbuilding crews (2) maintenance men, responsible for road upkeep and repair, replacement of lights, signs, guardrails; the trimming of boulevard lawns and hedges; clearing away litter, salting, sanding and clearing away snow in winter, roadwashing in spring (3) a security force (generally having full police powers) roamed the roads in unmarked vehicles, made spot checks and safety tests, ticketed speeders, transcribed accident details (4) ambulance and towtruck operators were stationed at regular intervals along the great routes, ready to come to the assistance of motorists in distress. Although not connected with the Department of Roads, the drivers of delivery vehicles — taxicabs, vans, 5-10 ton cartage trucks — as well made their living from, and spent most of their days on, the road.

But when the day was done, all these roadworkers could go home, put their feet up, greet their loved ones, relax, let the tension, the roar of the roadways fade away for a few well-earned, peaceful hours.

There was one type of fellow for whom this respite was denied, however, since he literally *lived* on the roads: the long-distance tractor-trailer driver. His cab was his home, equipped with a sleeper, air-conditioned, usually containing a tape deck, radio, t.v., a rollout table, freezer, and micro-oven: the necessities to sustain him as, daily, he rolled along the great routes.

A few got to know the feel and make of the roadways – each curve and hill, each biway and interchange – better than even the great roadbuilders themselves. But whatever the load, wherever the stop, the feeling of being outdoors, watching the world roll by, brought with it a sense of freedom an inside job never could. That, and the high pay, almost compensated for the loneliness. It was one of the toughest jobs there were, hard on the nerves, best suited to a rootless, restless breed of men anxious to be on the move. Even those who were married saw far too few days of the year at home.

But, in truck-stops or certain taverns, fellow truckers could be found to talk to about the roadways, other drivers, accidents they had seen or heard of – but usually the talk would come around to making it one day, owning a rig, maybe even starting up an outfit, retiring before sixty, before being left broke and alone, as happened to so many.

2.

JERAMIAH had gone a long way towards realizing just such a

dream, for he had recently acquired his own rig, christened her 'Marinda'. Marinda was a 'Fineline' Mach II diesel-combine sleeper, complete with all the extras; and now, almost at the end of her third run: she was carrying a load of perishables up from the south, via the West Coast Freeway, then east along the Transcontinental to the Mid-Capital.

It was 4:30. Marinda crawled along stop-and-go, in the midst of rush hour traffic. Jeramiah was tired, anxious to bed Marinda down, get some sleep himself. The Leslie Street exit which would carry him through the heart of the city and beyond, to Lakeshore Boulevard and the south depot of his company was still about 26 kilometres ahead.

He was, however, on the rim of a right-lane exit ramp. He couldn't make the streetsign out as he was directly beneath it. He calculated it would take 45 minutes to reach Leslie at the rate he was going. 'To hell with it. I'll take this ramp into the city, pick up an east road somewhere and cross over to Leslie.' He geared up, signalled, turned onto the ramp. 'Must be Victoria,' he thought, trying to recall the north-south artery prior to Leslie.

Jeramiah noted how smoothly this particular ramp curved up and around, how quickly it swept the traffic, the noise of the Transcontinental from view. It levelled out. It was long and unfamiliar. 'Hmm. Perhaps it is new. It's possible, of course.' He shifted into eighth. 'No traffic ... might be a better route down to the Lakeshore than Leslie ...'

The ramp ran smoothly towards the city. It was 4:45. Jeramiah glanced to his right. The sun was low; guardrail shadows extended over the road. Then he noticed there were no further streetlamps. 'That's it then. It *is* a new route, not yet completed. I'll ask Jack about it when I get in.' He glanced into Marinda's Texas benders. There were no cars behind, no end as yet in sight ahead. He frowned: 'I should be well down into the city by now. Must be a high ramp too, to overpass all other arteries ...' Although the ramp was unfamiliar, it was not surprising that it could be built quickly, for the roadbuilders could lay out and complete a roadway in a matter of weeks, and it had been several months since Jeramiah had been to Mid-Capital.

He began to look for an exit to Dundas, a main east-west city street. But there was no sign of any upcoming change. He shifted into ninth.

Ten minutes passed. His impatience turned, by degrees, to anger. 'Where the hell *does* this ramp come down? I'll be late getting in,' he muttered. He shifted into tenth, stepped on the gas. 'I've passed Dundas by now.' Puzzled, he drove on for awhile, then slowed down. Still no traffic. A ridiculous thought occurred to him; he laughed and dismissed it. Since his turn off the Transcontinental he had travelled 25 kilometres.

His anger gave way to disbelief mixed with a bit of fear. He considered turning back, eyeballed the width of the ramp. 'No, not on *this* stretch of road!' But he hadn't really considered it seriously, anyway.

It was almost sunset. The road ahead began to dim. 'This is silly,' he thought. He pulled over to the shoulder, shifted into neutral, pushed in his hazard button, pulled on his emergency brake, climbed out of the cab. The sight at the edge of the ramp startled him: a thick fog had rolled in below, level to the height of the ramp. The sun, also at the same level, was setting into the fog, casting cloudy shadows about him. He tried to look through it, but could see nothing; and, apart from the wind which churned through the clouds, there was no sound. 'But I should be able to hear *something!*' he thought. 'The city should be right below here! How high *is* this damn ramp anyway?' He sat on the guard rail, bewildered. 'Does this ramp span the entire city? It must. But a ramp that long? I would have heard about it – it's possible of course – it would have cost a fortune! But it isn't even necessary!' He stared down the empty road. Still no traffic. He tapped his fingers nervously on the guardrail. Marinda purred contentedly.

He considered turning around again – but it just wasn't possible. Nor could he uncouple the tractor without a fifth-wheel lock-wrench which only the hauling companies possessed – an innovation necessary due to a rising number of inter-city 'moonlight' hauls.

He couldn't risk climbing down the side of the ramp in the fog: he might be on a bridge or, as he suspected, a viaduct, similar to those on the West Lake Interchange. He could fall hundreds of feet.

But where did this ramp go? 'Perhaps it *is* a total overpass of the city. Maybe it slopes east, hooks up with the West Lake. Well, if it does, I can follow it around, enter the city that way ...' But it still didn't make any sense. 'No traffic. And no lights.' 'Weird!' It was like a t.v. spook show about another dimension, or something.

Jeramiah sat for a few moments more then climbed back into Marinda. 'There's nothing to do but go forward,' he thought. 'It's not the first time I've been lost, and it won't be the last; besides,' he smiled at his foolishness, 'the ramp will end shortly — so I've lost a little time, so what?'

The sun had set. His headlights beamed onto the roadway. It even occurred to him to stop the truck, *walk* back, though he had covered some 30-45 kilometres. But no. He was tired, it was a bit chilly, Marinda was warm and steady, sailing like a ship over a smooth grey sea. He drove on until too tired to think any more. Finally, having dulled his fear with exhaustion, he pulled over to the shoulder, lay down, immediately fell asleep.

3.

SUNLIGHT woke him. He lay easily staring into a cloudless sky. The events of the previous evening surfaced. He sat up, looked out along the ramp. 'I'll be able to get off now. The fog is gone. I'll climb down the gradient, find out where I am.'

He stood at the ramp's edge, astonished. Lanes and lanes of cars sped along below — so far below they appeared to be about one-quarter their actual size — he couldn't even hear them! These roadways stretched out to the horizon. He looked down to the edge of the ramp: there was *no* gradient! It was a viaduct then, the ramp supported by spans beneath.

He could *not* get down!

Suddenly he began to tremble, sat down on the guardrail, stared up at Marinda expectantly, as if she might provide an answer. He looked up and down the ramp, totally bewildered. 'Perhaps it is a dream – or maybe I *am* in 'the twilight zone' – on a ramp that will never end!'

He really didn't know what to do. He raised his hands, lowered them, looked around, sighed, even laughed a little. Just to hear the sound of his own voice he said: 'Still no traffic. All those cars down there and not a one here. Only so much gas. Only so much food – at least that load of fruit and vegetables is a lucky break ...' He sat on the guardrail trying to understand his strange situation, trying to remain calm. He crossed the ramp, looked over the other side: no, it had not been an hallucination; the lanes of traffic were there.

Again he thought of walking back. He estimated he had driven some 300 kilometres. It was so ridiculous it made him angry: 'This is REALLY STUPID!' he shouted, totally frustrated. Relieved of that, he forced himself to think further. Fear dictated walking back to be the better course, reason tempted him to continue. 'I could walk back but the ramp must end shortly; besides, it can't be supported at *all* points by spans! It must touch down *somewhere!* And he still had a second tank of gas which could carry him many kilometres, effortlessly, in a few hours. To walk back would take 3 or 4 days, maybe more. But it was pride which decided the issue: he would appear a fool to his superiors, his friends, other truckers, if they ever found out he had gotten lost, abandoned his truck, walked back so far — he would never be able to live it down — likely this ramp was common knowledge to them all, everyone knew about it but him!

'Actually,' Jeramiah thought, 'it is ridiculous to think one is in a "twilight zone".' He had to laugh. One had to have a sense of humour about things. Odd things happened to people every day — odd, not unreal. No need to get upset, or panic. With more than a full tank of gas he would be able to cover the remaining distance that very afternoon!

He climbed back into Marinda, but as he drove along he could not help considering the worst: the ramp might not end before his fuel ran out — a silly idea of course but — to avoid this unpleasant prospect for as long as possible, he cruised at around 90 kph, in order to burn a minimum amount of fuel and obtain maximum mileage.

'... And if Marinda runs out of gas, I'll have to walk. What shall I carry with me? Flashlight, knife, fruit — those canned apricots — some lettuce. Hmm. I'll make a knapsack out of my blanket. There's rope somewhere in the trailer. Now what else ...'

In midafternoon, the first tank empty, Jeramiah switched to tank 2. Occasionally he pulled over to the shoulder: the countryside below had changed — more farmland, the roadways were less numerous — but the height and structure of the ramp remained the same: he could not get down.

Late that afternoon it began to rain. The close, heavy clouds pressed in upon him, made him feel as though he were in some sort of no-man's land, lost from any reality he had ever known.

Fear kept him going. He drove all night. The rain continued. The steady, slick hum of Marinda's tires slipping over the wet road, the monotonous swish of the windshield wipers had a soothing, almost hypnotic effect on him. He stared dumbly along the path the headlights carved out of the night. He rarely looked down the roadway now for a sign of change.

In a fogbound dawn Marinda, out of gas, coasted quietly to a halt. Jeramiah tried the engine a couple of times — in vain. He sat for a long time watching the mist and rain shift about, slowly film his windshield. Now and then he turned the wipers on to clear the windows, just for something to do. All was quiet, save for an intermittent wind which flattened against Marinda's side. Finally Jeramiah simply lay down, pulled his blanket around him, and slept.

For three days he stayed with Marinda. He had plenty of food, the cab sheltered him from the wet weather, which continued. He knew he had to come to terms with his situation: going back was out of the question. What lay ahead? On the third day the sky cleared, the sun was warm, inviting, Jeramiah decided to accept the invitation.

He had as well considered the possibility that he might die on that bizarre roadway which apparently led nowhere, had no end. 'Perhaps I'm *already* dead, this is my fate, to search for the end of this roadway forever.' — But he doubted it. He vowed he would fight, continue on for as long as he could.

It took him most of the afternoon to convert his blanket

into a knapsack with the help of a little rope. Once finished, he filled it with canned apricots, several heads of lettuce, flashlight and batteries, a knife, some tools, looped it over his shoulder. He was ready to go. 'Well, I dont know whether I'll see you again or not, my Marinda. You've been a swell lady.' He patted her fender gently. 'Goodbye, Marinda.' He started off down the road. When next he looked back, she was out of sight.

He walked a slow, steady pace, and at first, muscles grown lazy from lack of use complained about the extra work. He ate a few leaves of lettuce, half a can of apricots a day. It was not at all unpleasant at first: it was summer, warm, the weather held. He thought of winter a couple of times but shrugged it off: he'd be long gone before then unless ... He checked the ramp edge often; although the landscape below continued to change, it remained inaccessible.

On the fifteenth day after leaving Marinda he spotted a car ahead, to the side of the ramp. As he came closer he saw it had long been abandoned; rusted frame, flat tires. Yet it gave him hope. 'At least someone – perhaps more than one – is ahead – somewhere – unless ...'

He examined the car. Anything of use had been taken. He found ownership papers in the glove compartment: Stanley Belding, 5711 Levelle Crescent, Central Square, Fd.

The car was a standard minimodel which ran on solar batteries to about 50 kph, automatically switched to gasoline for higher speeds. But batteries when used continually burnt out quickly, and the gas wouldn't last long. 'so he got this far – but why didn't he turn back? Makes no sense. I wonder if he's still alive ...'

He spent the day by the car relaxing. He ate lunch sitting on the guardrail looking out over the land: the roadways had diminished until now only a single lane weaved in and out amongst farmlands – farmlands which reminded him of his childhood home. And he felt as frightened as a lost child would, alone in a strange land. No longer could he reach down and touch the earth, and perhaps he never would be able to again. That thought affected him deeply, touched off all he had been feeling since this strange journey had begun, and he began to cry. It relieved him to release his feelings, and that night he slept more soundly than he had for some time.

He dreamt of his father chopping logs for a fence for their garden in Central West. 'Can I help?' he asked. 'No son. You stay back now. This is dangerous work.' Disappointed, Jeramiah watched. But, seeing that his son wanted to do something, his father said 'How about carrying some of these chips to the house, give them to your ma for the fire?' Delighted, Jerry picked up a few chips, ran to the house. The house! Suddenly the memory of his home, intact in every detail, unfolded within him; and there in the doorway stood his mother. 'I see you've brought some wood! How nice! Is your father busy?...'

Jeramiah woke at this point. It was early morning. The vivid dream filled him with a contentment he had not felt in years. A little later on he continued down the ramp, ready for whatever fate might lay ahead.

On the thirty-first day he ate the last bit of food. Two days later it rained heavily. He caught a chill, for he had no way to keep dry, or to dry out. The chill caused his temperature to rise, made him thirsty. He drank heavily from his stock of water, but the fever did not abate. He began to feel dizzy, unsteady on his feet. 'It's beginning now,' he thought. 'Death will have its way.' Now more than ever his eyes strained ahead, looking for some sign, some indication of change, however trivial; but there was nothing: the pavement unrolled steadily the same, as it had done from the beginning.

He used the guardrail to steady himself. He tried hard to concentrate simply on moving, for his mind began to drift to other things; unrelated topics and thoughts began to mix and muddle. It became difficult to focus on anything specific. To fight this confusion he began to speak out loud, tried to focus on the sound of his words. But the fever was too strong. His speech became incoherent, raving.

The fever increased. He began to hallucinate. He thought he saw a pile of wood chips by the roadside, pointed at it, laughed. He imagined cool streaming water, a shallow pool in warm sunlight ... an image of Marinda, the woman he once loved, smiled at him briefly, then this image too became confused, jumbled, changed to another ...

The images became more real to him than his surroundings. He cut his hand on the tin guardrail but did not feel it, or notice it bleeding. Nor did he see, when he gazed out over the guardrail, a crystal-blue lake, its gentle waves lapping along the edge of the ramp.

It was the thirty-seventh day, about noon. He took one more step. It was his last. He paused, swayed. Just before he fell, he thought he saw something, but then drifted into darkness.

No more than 45 metres away a small canvass tent sat neatly by the roadside, clearly within his view.

4.

HE AWOKE looking into the face of a young woman.

'Ah! You've come out of it!'

Jeramiah, only partially conscious, stared at her.

'You've been unconscious almost a week. I really didn't think you'd make it – you were shivering so, your teeth chattering, lips blue – and quite delirious.' She brought a cup of hot broth to his lips. 'Here, drink this.'

The warm liquid felt as though it was the best thing he had ever tasted. He made an effort to move but was too weak. He looked up at his benefactor dreamily; she had blue eyes, gold hair, a dark tan. He fell asleep.

He woke late that night. The woman lay sleeping a few metres away. As his mind cleared, he realized that he had been rescued, and that they were in a tent. His strength having returned he rose, moved across the tent, folded the tent flap aside, steped out into the warm night air and onto – the ramp. He stood for a long while, disappointed, confused, wondering indeed if the whole thing was a dream: it was too real – and too unreal – at the same time. 'Well, at least I'm alive,' he thought. He became conscious of the sound of water. He stumbled over to the guardrail. The moon carved a path towards him over the still waters of – a lake! Moon and stars dipped and floated about in the dark waters. It was too much. Suddenly he felt quite exhausted by his efforts. Too tired to think about anything at all, still a bit weak, he returned to the tent – and to sleep.

In the morning a gentle nudge woke him.

'Hi.' she smiled.

'Hi.' Jeramiah sat up, looked at her. She was very attractive.

'Well thanks,' he said. 'You saved my life.'

'You're welcome. I'm glad you're better.'

'What's your name?'

'Azure. Yours?'

'Jeramiah. Tell me, how long you been here?'

'A year or so. I stopped trying to keep track after awhile – too many other things to do.' She studied him for a moment. 'You sure you're all right?'

'I feel o.k.'

'All right then. I guess I'll tell you how I got here – I'll tell you my story then you tell me yours. O.k.?'

'O.k.'

'Stan and I were going camping – must've been about this time last year. I had spent the day packing and loading his car, and was on my way to pick him up when it happened.

'I was driving along the Transcontinental during rush

hour – about 4:30 I guess, Stan worked at Cleever's, at Leslie and Orchard Park Drive. I'd intended to turn off at Leslie, but traffic was heavy, and it looked as though I was going to be late. I was alongside an exit ramp – this ramp – decided to take it south for a bit then cut over to Leslie. Well, you know the rest. Certainly I wouldn't be alive today but for the food supply and camping gear.'

'But why didn't you turn back?'

'Yeah. Wish I could have. You saw the car?'

'Yes.'

'It's a new minimodel – the 'Axis' it was called – with the wheel-lock conrols? You know, the lock control is supposed to disengage automatically when you start the car. Well, this one began to stick. I don't know why. Some defect, I guess. Anyway, the car wouldn't turn more than a quarter turn either way; I could drive straight ahead – that was all.'

'– And your reverse didn't work, right?'

'Right. It would go into reverse gear all right, but it wouldn't move – as though I had the emergency brake on – how'd you know?'

'I remember that car – it was a defect. Last year some 200,000 were recalled for just that adjustment. Reverse and the lock system had a tendency to jam when in a certain position. Yours must've been one of those on recall.'

'Anyway, why didn't you walk back, then?'

'Ha! Why didn't *you?*' she smiled. 'Likely the same reason. I kept thinking the damn ramp would *end!* But it just never did. I kept driving, and after three days the battery gave out

– I *had* to keep it running then, so I drove nonstop until the gas gave out. Then I walked – as I presume you did – until I came to this lake and the ramp started to slope down. At this point I could reach the water. So, I'd come this far. I decided to stay right here for awhile. And here I've stayed. I made a few trips back and forth to the car to bring up the camping equipment. I know I can't make it the distance back on foot – so I decided a couple of weeks ago to move on ahead, at least see how far the lake goes, how long I'll have access to it. You're lucky. A few more days and I wouldn't have been here to find you.' She smiled again. She was about to add something, then changed her mind. 'Anyway let's go outside,' she finally said. 'It's stuffy in here.'

Jeramiah was astonished to see – by the side of the tent – a garden!

'Yes,' she said. 'I'll explain that.' They sat down on the guardrail, and she continued: 'After I'd set up the tent, rested up, settled in – I took a swim in the lake, found it's only about a metre-and-a-half or so deep, with a muddy bottom.

'But my main problem, of course, was food. I still had a bit of the food I'd taken from the car, but not much: a few eggs, juice, canned fruit, potatoes, onions. Not enough to last very long. Some of the potatoes had already begun to rot, so I threw them by the side of the road. After a few days I had an idea – it was a longshot really – I spent – I don't know how many days – scooping mud from the lakebed, spreading it out until I had enough for this garden. During this time I lived on fresh water and watercress. I planted some of the onions, some potato eyes, and prayed. The soil, as you can see, is quite rich. I've had a full crop this year. The lake is full of fish – when you go for a swim you'll see them all around you. Stan's fishing rod was in the car; and there were still some canned goods in the trunk. When I felt strong enough, I went back for them, brought back some tools as well. I'd never fished before, but this sort of situation requires that one learn quickly, and I did. They bite at just about anything that moves. There are numerous water beatles along the shoreline – which aren't too bad fried – and I used them for bait. Fish love them.

'Anyway, that's about it – oh, we also have fire. The wooden guardrail stumps burn easily. Among the tools I had packed a hatchet which I use to cut the stumps into chips. I have a pair of glasses which I had to wear while driving – I simply focus the sun onto the chips – they catch fire quickly. – Don't look so surprised. After all, I didn't have anything *else* to do. I could either panic – and do nothing – or think of ways to survive; the latter seemed the more productive of the two options. It became a kind of a game, really, me against the elements, only certain materials, and so on. It was even enjoyable at times. – Moreso, I'm sure, than panic and probably death would have been.

'Oh yes, one more thing. Remember I told you I threw some rotted potatoes away? Well, I threw parts of fish onto the same pile, and damned if some sort of yeast didn't start growing out of it! When you're hungry, of course, you'll try anything. I sampled a bit of it, allowed time for digestion, sampled a bit more. It's not bad. It has kind of a nutty flavour. I expect it's packed with protein, and it is one of my staples as well. I mix it regularly into my onion and potato soups!'

'Whew! That's quite an incredible story! Most people would not have been nearly so resourceful!'

Azure laughed. 'Oh sure! Don't forget I'm settled in *now!* But you should've seen me *then!* I guess I'm making it sound far more calm and rational than it actually was – it was a struggle every inch of the way, for sure – and of course, it's not over! – But now, that's enough of me. Tell me about you.'

Jeramiah told his tale, and by the time he had finished it was midday.

Azure had piled little stores of wood chips at various locations along the ramp. The two of them gathered some and Jeramiah watched as Azure made the fire. She had, as well, a pot, a pan, some plates, knives and forks, and a grill. She told him she had made another trip back to the car that spring for utensils and whatever else she could find. She placed the pot on the grill over the fire and in an hour they had some yeast/onion soup.

'Very tasty,' Jeramiah said. 'My compliments to the chef.'

'Thank you. It's nice to have someone to share it with.'

A week later, as Azure had planned, they packed everything together and moved down the ramp. The lake remained level with the ramp for about 250 kilometres then gradually began to fall away. They travelled a few more kilometres then decided to settle in for winter, which they hoped would be mild, since they were much further south.

Jeramiah asked Azure how she had made it through the previous winter.

'It wasn't easy. I kept a fire going most of the time from the supply of wood I'd gathered during the fall. I boiled water over the fire and lived on a 'diet' of hot soup for 4 months. There was one bad stretch of several weeks during which the temperature dropped well below freezing. I'd just wrap my sleeping bag around myself, huddle by the fire – those were the hardest days I've had ...'

They went about setting up the garden again, and when winter did come, it was indeed mild. Azure spent the days preparing food and tending the fire; Jeramiah fished and chopped wood. And so they lived.

They got on well, were soon good friends. At first they talked about their lives in the residential and industrial sectors, lives which bore few similarities to their present situation. To a certain extent they had adjusted to life on the ramp. Although the work was hard, it was satisfying; the pace of daily life was slower, more relaxed than the old ways had allowed for; they had the time and opportunity to get in touch with the self within, as it related to the world without: not an hysterical, mechanized world but the world *as it really was:* flexible, organic, filled with colour and beauty, and above all, with mystery. Although the earth itself was out of reach, the grand, white clouds; sky and sun; the fresh, light wind which blew steadily across the lake – daily washed them in colours and sights, motions and sounds. They talked at great length about these 'two,' almost diametrically opposed, worlds: man's unsuccessful attempt to *dominate* the world by rendering it 'reasonable,' separating from rather than uniting with; in contrast to man's place *within* the world, uniting with rather than separating from.

But such topics exhausted themselves as their friendship grew warmer, expanded, by degrees, into a feeling of care for one another, respect and love.

In spring they ventured beyond the security of the lake — beyond their food and water supply — determined to search out the ramp's end. Beyond the lakeshore bare, rocky hills, gravelled slopes, ragweed and sand quickly dwindled into desert; after roughly 100 kilometres this scenario changed again to grassland, trees, other roadways, far below.

On this particular section of ramp a lichen grew to about 5 centimetres thickness. It was edible raw, fried, tasted good in soups, and the yeast they had developed went well with it. Although fish were no longer available for their yeast, they found their distilled urine plus potato rot produced it just as well. Yeast and lichen became their staple diet. They experimented with the lichen until they learned its proper growth conditions — (cool air and a bit of moisture) which enabled them to carry it with them. Piled deeply enough the lichen also provided sufficient nutrients to replenish their dwindling supply of potatoes and onions.

They moved steadily along the ramp. That year, Azure had her first child; and as their search for the end of the ramp continued, the little family grew larger. Years began to pass them by.

ONE DAY, towards the end of the day, Jeramiah's eldest son, Mark, came to him and said 'Father, tell us about the ramp.'

Jeramiah smiled, surprised. 'All right Mark,' he said. 'Go get your brothers and sisters and bring them here.'

Azure began to prepare some stew for the evening meal over a fire as the children gathered around.

5.

'SOME TIME AGO, there was a lofty civilization which built great buildings and contemplated grand designs. This civilization consisted of complex industrial sectors and living or 'residential' sectors. The purpose of industrial sectors was to provide anything which anyone could ever want, instantly; residential sectors allowed for the necessary leisure time to consume whatever goods or services one might choose.

'Instant' availability, however, necessitated a very sophisticated transportation system: commodities might arrive by plane, ship, or train, but ultimately it was via the road that they would finally be delivered.

'So it was that Ramos, the Great Architect, initiated and built the Tanscontinental Highway, a roadway system extending from one end of the land to the other, its ramps and biways going everywhere, so that no segment of the continent, however remote, need ever feel deprived of anything.

'And once the Transcontinental was completed, it appeared that everyone was satisfied. Utopia had become a reality; the perfect, complete society had been achieved. For surely if everyone has everything one wants, well then, what more could one ask for? If you had all you wished for, Marinda, would you then wish for even more?'

'No papa.'

'Yet, human nature is a strange thing, children. The truth was people were *not* satisfied.

'Even during my day, the works of Ramos had been challenged. It seemed that flaws had been found, problems had arisen which Ramos and his men had not foreseen. Why, it was even suggested in some quarters that his entire system was out-of-date! New, more-super freeways were built, their arms reaching out over truly incredible distances. Ramps became longer, higher, stretched ever-farther across the face of the Western World. And why? Why, so things could be even *more* instantly available than before!

'Often workmen on a ramp site did not know where they were building a ramp to, or when a project might end. Some lived right on the ramp site, much as we live on this one, built fires on the dry cement as we do, set up tents similar to ours. Unlike us, of course, they could always return to the earth and their homes. Why, I even heard of cases where some men lived, worked, and died on a site without ever knowing its destination, without ever seeing the completion of the project towards which the fruits of their lifelong labours had been directed.

'YET, even *this* was not enough! Talk had begun of building an Intercontinental Roadway, a roadway so vast it would span the oceans, include industrial and residential 'pods' run on wave-energy, allowing man to tap the resources of ocean floors. Such a roadway would continue out (so its designers claimed) over European and Asian soils, spread and multiply until roadways covered the Eastern Hemisphere at least as effectively as they did in the West. The spread of Western civilization into Europe and the East was considered necessary, since the goods at home were running out. In order to supply everythng to everyone instantly — the West had effectively consumed itself. Indeed, some observers believed that in fact *no one* wanted everything instantly, and since the West had systematically destroyed itself to promote goals which no one wanted, grounds could be found to support the premise that irrational — or at the very least, incomplete — motivations on the part of that community was shortly to cause its demise.

'Whatever the case might be, there was a great deal of objection forthcoming from European and Asian countries: they foresaw the West sucking their lands dry as well, in spite of Western protestations that they would not do so, that an Intercontinental Roadway would raise the standard of living around the world, would necessarily be of benefit to all.

'But the West had a strong economic hold on many European countries; such countries were not in a position to refuse to bargain; others hedged, not wanting to offend, yet finding the prospect of Western intervention extremely undesirable.

'The strongest objections arose from countries (many Asian) within which the West had no influence at all. As all countries had tactical nuclear weapons, the West could not entirely disregard such objections. Of course the West could easily annihilate such trifling opponents (and considered doing so), but most agreed that to do so would be like lighting a match in a powder room. Nor was it likely that economic boycotts would be effective in such cases, for nations opposed to Western policies had many friends – admittedly or otherwise.

'The leaders of these few resisting nations told the world that they were prepared to go to *any* lengths to preserve their way of life – their cultural, intellectual, and spiritual heritage – from absorption and ultimately extinction. To them, the West appeared a monsterous glutton, hoarding and wasting vast quantities of material wealth, stuffing itself to the bursting-point rather than sharing its bounty with those less fortunate. They were unimpressed by the millions of tons of relief foods, grains and wheats which were sent abroad, regarded such gestures as political manoeuvres designed to instill dependency, to gain support for Western expansionist policies. When they looked to the Western continent itself, what they saw there was an abhorrence to them: 'Better annihilation through war than capitulation to the jaws of the West!' One leader proclaimed. 'At least in war we have a chance!' Such strong words – backed by nuclear arms — had to be heeded.

'How it was resolved — *if* it was resolved — I don't know, for it was about that time I stumbled onto this ramp. That was the world from which your father and mother came.'

Jeramiah paused for a moment, then said 'But you asked me to tell you about this ramp, which grew out of that world:

OF YOU, my children, I ask one thing *only:* there is only one law on this ramp: to continue to follow it. Sooner or later it will end, and then you will come to experience the world as it is — for better or for worse — I have no idea what it will be like wherever this ramp descends. But you will see animals, feel cool grass beneath your feet, smell flowers, experience the beauty of the earth, talk to other men and women, make friends, live in a home rooted in earth, not up here, suspended on a cold cement platform. Perhaps someday, when we stretch ourselves outwards into the solar system, perhaps beyond, things will be different; until then, this is the only sanity I can see ...

'But yes, this is the only thing: continue to follow the ramp. Remember that I tell it to you. Of all the things I have or will tell you, it is *this* which is the most important of all.'

'But why, father?' Mark asked.

'Because to continue down the ramp is to have hope for a better future, for the end of something old, the beginning of something new; to stop and wait can only result in despair, for it is an end to searching. You might look back along the ramp from time to time to see where you have been, but do so whimsically, children, not with a longing to return, for such a longing too, invites despair.

'And be easy on yourselves children, be kind to yourselves and to each other. Be curious about one another, seek out and encourage what is new and different in each of you and keep that spark alive; discover what excites your passions, where you agree and disagree; respect those differences between yourselves, encourage them; allow for that flexibility of expression. That way life won't be so 'hard' on you. If one accepts that contradictions and differences need not be resolved or forever settled, life becomes simpler – a 'softer' proposition, more likely to be a joyful experience than a painful one.'

Pause.

'Well! I'm glad you asked me to tell you about the ramp, Mark. It has certainly brought up a lot of thoughts and feelings I didn't even know I had! – And it has answered some important questions for you: now you have some understanding of where you came from.

'It is all the knowledge I have of the days we've left behind.'

Jeramiah leaned back, silent. The fire crackled lazily in front of them. His family was silent too, thoughtful about what he said about the ramp, and the world beyond its rim.

During the next few days his children asked him many questions concerning these and other things, and he answered them as best he could. And after a time they were satisfied. Their interests turned to other things. They had various tasks to do as the family moved slowly along the ramp.

But they remembered what their father had said, as he

had asked of them, and spoke of these things amongst themselves from time to time.

THE RAMP CONTINUED ON, Jeramiah and Azure grew old, and one day, as they were crossing a particularly cool stretch of road, Jeramiah fell ill, a victim to the delirious chill which had struck him in his youth. It took hold of him quickly, and four days later he passed away in Azure's arms. Minutes before his death his delirium passed, and with clear eyes he looked up at the woman he loved, and smiled; then closed his eyes for the last time.

His family buried him in a mound of lichen by the side of the ramp. They spent the day by his resting place, then, obeying the dictum Jeramiah himself had set, moved along the ramp.

Mark assumed leadership. Azure found it increasingly difficult to maintain the daily pace, but said nothing of it. One day, exhausted, she fell, and was unable to get up. The boys made a stetcher out of tin and cloth and carried her for months.

She passed away early one morning while her children slept. She woke to see the sun rise on what promised to be a grand day. Her last thoughts were of Jeramiah.

The children assumed the tasks of their parents, and their children did so as well. Generations of the sons and daughters of Jeramiah and Azure continued on down the ramp searching, ever searching, for its end.

6.

IT WAS a warm night in late summer. Noren looked out over grasslands to a forest wall a few kilometres ahead. The community stood behind him, silent. For the first time they heard the sound of wind passing through grass and leaves, and smelt the rich, thick scent of earth.

Several days prior to that evening the ramp had suddenly begun to narrow and descend on a slow but steady arc, until at its lip, where it met the earth, it measured little more than two metres in width. Beyond the lip a gravel path extended for a few metres then vanished into grass. There in the still night, moonlight changing and fading about them, the little company stood, awestruck and silent.

Finally Noren turned to everyone and said: 'This is a truly momentous event. The Council will meet in the morning. We must talk amongst ourselves, pray Ramos will guide us well as we consider what to do.'

Talor stood outside his tent. He found it hard to contain his joy on this occasion – but knew he had to. More than once before he had seen what happened to those who disobeyed the Laws of Ramos: banishment back down the ramp, a banishment to Despair.

Perhaps it was true that without the boundaries of the ramp one would become lost, fragmented, drown in the Chaos of the world; yet in spite of that frightening possibility Talor wanted to jump up, yell, run and bounce out into the grass, roll around in it! Perhaps, as some said, he was mad. He didn't know about that. He only knew what he felt inside.

He had long had the reputation of being somewhat rebellious, neglectful of his tasks, given to daydreaming or prone to wandering off down the ramp ahead, where he would remain for long hours lost in thought. It was true enough that he interpreted the Laws of Ramos differently from his fellows, but, for fear of banishment, he had kept his thoughts mostly to himself – save for Eilana, his woman. To her he revealed his heart, for he knew she loved him, would not betray him, no matter how strange his thoughts might seem.

The gathering was dispersing. Eilana came to him. 'Why don't you look?' she said.

'I already have,' Talor mumbled. 'I was here last week."

'Oh, Talor! You were the first, then! But you said nothing!'

'Of course not. I was afraid of trouble with the Council. You know how I feel about them – and how they feel about me!'

'Yes, I know.' She looked at him quizzically: 'But you're upset. What is it?'

He gestured towards the gathering – 'This. Everyone standing around so solemn, fearful. It should be a moment of joy! It is a liberation, time for a celebration! For the first time, the world is at our feet! What could be more beautiful, more exciting? – But no. We must wait. Consider. Do this. Do that. For what?'

'But Talor, we need to make some plans. We can't just run about all over. There must be *some* sort of order –'

Talor frowned. 'Now you talk like them.'

'But what's the harm in waiting for just a little while? It's so new ...'

'I know. I'm a bit frightened too. But I'm more frightened of what the Council has in mind.'

'What do you mean?'

'I feel uneasy about all these deliberations – now another meeting tomorrow. I don't know. It's just a feeling, that's all. I'll be talking to Noren in the morning. I guess I'll find out what he has in mind then.'

Eilana stared into the fire in front of their hut. 'Talor,' she said slowly, 'I'll go with you – you know that – wherever you wish to go ... Maybe my reason is clouded by love,' she smiled. 'Perhaps you *are* a fool as some say – I don't know; it doesn't really matter what others think – I guess you're sane enough for me.'

For the first time that day Talor laughed.

The next day he went to see Noren.

'What shall we do?' he asked the elder.

'We'll wait for a few days,' Noren replied. 'Allow people to get used to the idea.'

'– You know that to Wait is against the Law.'

'Yes. But then, Talor, you were never one who had much respect for the Law, isn't that so?'

'No, it *isn't* so. I have always felt the Laws were good – so long as they applied. Once inapplicable, however, they hinder that which most they propose to help – the law aids the crime it wishes to remedy.'

'An interesting theory. But it is the people who must change the law, come to recognize its faults of their own accord.'

'All right Noren. And as a person it is my opinion that the Laws of Ramos are, as of yesterday, not only void, but harmful to our future development.'

'There are those who would disagree with you.'

'They're mistaken.'

'You're a very arrogant young man, Talor.'

'And you're a dull old conservative,' Talor thought. Impatient, he said 'Yes, yes you're right. But look, you know the Laws of Ramos as well as I: 'To Wait is to give up Hope; to Go Back is to enter into Despair; to Continue along the ramp is to Hope. Thus spoke Jeramiah!' he quoted. And those laws were good so long as the ramp continued. The ramp has ended, and so the Laws no longer hold.'

'It is not that simple Talor.'

'Oh, great skies, Noren!' Talor exclaimed, unable to contain his frustration, 'the search is over!'

'All right Talor, since you know everything, tell me, how are we to proceed?'

'Proceed?' Talor shrugged. 'Simple. Go out, settle. Do much as we are doing now, only we'll have the world to settle in, rather than just a thin strip of cement.'

'And in which direction should we go?'

'Does it matter?'

'It might. This is what we are discussing in Council. We are afraid of the dissolution of the community: people wandering off, getting lost, or even going Back.'

'— But surely if we stay together —'

'Yes, but we really don't know what will happen, do we? Besides, we're together now. Look, Talor, I am the leading elder. I have watched this community grow and flourish during my time. We are happy here. Everyone is content — although there are a few in each generation like yourself, who, for whatever reasons, seem to be discontent no matter *what* changes are made! You must see this as well from the point of view of others, not just your own. Why risk Chaos? You are not the only one faced with a decision about this.'

'But *I* am the only one who can make *my* decision. The decision of the community is not my problem.'

'It is if you wish to stay with this community.'

'What you are saying is that in order to stay with it I must put the interests of everyone else before my own! Then tell me, Noren, in what way can I contribute something of myself to it? You want everybody to be a 'yes' man to Council decisions, that's what I think.' He paused. 'What do you have in mind for me Noren, if I don't agree? Banishment?'

Noren sighed. 'No, Talor. You haven't done anything against the Law. But you don't understand.'

'All right, all right. What *do* you intend to do then?'

'Obey the Laws of Ramos.'

Talor laughed. '*That* should be interesting. Just how do you intend to do that? You cannot Wait and you cannot Go Back without breaking the law; nor can you Continue, since there is no longer a ramp to follow.'

'You are mistaken. We *shall* obey the Law. We have the

men, the know-how, and the equipment ...'

Talor stared at Noren for a moment, puzzled; then realized what he meant: 'Y-You – oh, Skies, you can't be serious!' He leaned over the small desk, looked intently into the old man's face: 'Are you seriously telling me you intend to-to- *build* the ramp so that you can continue to follow it?'

Noren nodded.

'You're mad!' Talor exploded. 'It's OVER, I tell you. The ramp has ended! For Skies' sake, IT'S RIGHT IN FRONT OF YOUR EYES!! The world is out there, waiting for us to enjoy!'

'ENOUGH!' Noren shouted angrily, smashed his fist on the desk. 'I've tried to be patient with you but I've had *enough* of you for one day! Now you listen, and listen well: it is the decision of the Council. Since the ramp began to narrow, we have been discussing it. There will be a general meeting and announcement tonight. Rumors of the decision are already circulating. Most of our people are agreeable to this proposal. It is the best way to keep the Law. And if you don't obey the Law, Talor, you *know* the penalty! Work will begin next week, and *you* will work along with everyone else! Now that is all there is to say about it! Good day!'

A week later, work began: large, flat bricks were made from a clay-mud mixture which was gathered from the edges of the ramp. It was generally agreed that should the terrain change, other means could always be found to enable them to Continue.

And Talor worked as well, since the alternative would

have been Banishment Back down the ramp. But as he worked he waited. He told Eilana what he was going to do. At first she objected to his plan. It frightened her. But finally she agreed.

One evening, while the camp slept, they slipped over the edge of the ramp, slid down an earthy slope into tall, cool grass. At first they thought it was the end for them; the earth seemed so soft compared to the hard cement they had always lived on they felt they would be swallowed up, keep going down – perhaps into Chaos. Shakily, they stood up.

'Strange, eh?'

'Yes.'

'– Come on,' he said, taking her hand, 'to the forest. Don't Wait.' Talor experienced a momentary panic which surprised him: he hadn't allowed for the shock of suddenly being without the security of the ramp. The realization that they could go anywhere, in any direction they chose, made him feel giddy, a bit frightened. 'C'mon!' he repeated. They ran across the field.

At the edge of the forest – somewhat intimidated by the dark trees which reached so high above them – they paused, looked back towards the ramp. Fires lit up the huts which until a few moments ago they had called home.

'We could always go back ...' Eilana murmured.

Talor smiled. 'We can never go back now.' He turned to her and said: 'I love you very much. You are very brave.'

'No,' she suddenly began to cry, 'I am afraid."

They walked into the forest.

But Talor had not been alone in his thoughts, only more vocal. Others followed. One day Talor and Eilana met some old friends. It was a happy reunion. Here and there families banded together, little villages formed.

Even a few of the oldest generation left the ramp, carried with them various tales and legends of how the ramp began, passed them on to the young, that they might know from whence they came.

And there were many as well who continued on building the ramp, through grass and snow, forest lands and mountain country, around lakes and over foreign lands, content to fish and forage from its confines, obeying the Laws of Ramos until the end of their days.